HAMPSHIRE COUNTRY WAYS

Country Ways

HAMPSHIRE
AND THE ISLE OF WIGHT

by Anthony Howard

Halsgrove in association with Meridian Broadcasting

MERIDIAN

First published in 1999 by Halsgrove

ISBN 1 841140 13 9

Cataloguing in Publication Data

A CIP record for this title is available from the British Library

HALSGROVE
Publishing, media and distribution
Halsgrove House
Lower Moor Way
Tiverton
Devon EX16 6SS

Tel: 01884 243242
Fax: 01884 243325
www.halsgrove.com

Main front cover picture: *Old Mill House on the River Anton, Fullerton.* Terry Heathcote.

Printed in Great Britain by Redwood Books, Trowbridge

CONTENTS

Introduction

Few people in the world are so unlucky that they have no place which is special to them. And those who are that unfortunate are unhappy indeed. The southern coastal counties of England enclose more than their fair share of such places, and those who live in the South have a richness of choice denied to most other human beings. Even with the maelstrom of the motorways, the horrors of Heathrow and Gatwick and the impertinent invasion of privacy of the Channel Tunnel, this is still countryside to cherish. It is no coincidence that people from all over Britain, and from further afield, yearn to come and make their homes in Kent and Sussex, Wiltshire and Berkshire, Dorset, Hampshire and Surrey.

It is not only in the summer, spring and autumn that the South Country casts its spell. Even in the dog days of January and February there is plenty of beauty, solitude and peace to discover along the coastline counties. All seasons have their charms and their challenges and the secret of finding them is to take your courage in your hands, to forswear the main roads and the known ways and to travel the tracks and lanes and paths of Old England. Then you will meet people the like of whom you have never met before, find rivers and streams which you did not know existed, visit villages which are not marked on any map, and enjoy views which few before you have seen.

Something of the sort happened to that great chronicler of the English downland, H.J. Massingham, when he climbed Butser Hill, beside Petersfield on the borders of Hampshire and Sussex, in the 1930s. This nine-hundred-foot giant of the South Downs has seen history ebb and flow across its slopes from the primeval downsmen through neolithic and Bronze ages, to the Romans and on to the present day. Massingham wrote:

There is much more to its nine hundred feet than to serve as man's tablet to scrawl his chequered annals on. If Butser is one of the books of early man, it would be as precious were its pages blank. Its surpassing beauty derives partly from its pose among the environing hills and partly from its conformation. No fewer than eight spurs with almost headlong coombes between them taper down from the circular plateau and make it the starfish of the southern hills. The flanks of these coombes are, most of them, mantled in trees, and the south-eastern spur in a yew forest most venerable, with silver-flashing whitebeam and the green turf about it to darken the shades yet deeper. But the grey-green plateau itself is bare, except for patches of primeval scrub – bowed and knotted thorn, huddled furze and juniper stiffly formal in design and yet the wildest of all the wild growths in England. These stray locks in no way obstruct the lines of Butser's Titan head – at once so elemental and so finished. They are in tune with an antiquity so great that the hill-grass was browsed by a million generations of herbivores before it was pressed by the foot of man. It is on the winds of Butser that floats the consolation of those words, 'As it was in the beginning, is now and ever shall be'. The scorings of ancient man have creased this Samson's limbs and shoulders, while man of today has peeled strips of their skin for his tennis-lawns. Yet Butser's head will still be raised over the hills of the east and west when rebel man is no more.

So what is it that makes the South of England so special? It is hard to argue that there are not equally beautiful and many more dramatic places to visit in the rest of England and in Scotland, Ireland, Wales and, of course, the rest of Europe and the world. It is difficult to pretend that much of the beauty of the place has not been threatened and in some cases destroyed by overcrowding, traffic, civilian and military aircraft, selfish farming, dreadful building decisions and human stupidity. And yet there is still a unique and civilised atmosphere in these southern counties which offers comfort and security to those lucky enough to live here. It has something to do with the area being part of a country which has not been successfully invaded since 1066. That, in turn, has a lot to do with being an island, a status which has been compromised by the digging of the Channel Tunnel. Whatever the material benefits and however great the engineering achievement, the fact of being joined to the Continent will certainly have a psychological influence on the people of Britain and of the South in particular.

An important part of the special nature of these counties is created by the Downs, both North and South. Nothing quite like them exists anywhere else in the world and, in a region without mountains, they offer high ground and views which are second to none. In addition, the South Downs make up a magnificent and secure barrier against the sea and its cursing winter winds as well as the fear of foreign invasion. All of us, since the birth of man, have seemed to need an edge to live against, and the Downs provide such a comfort for the whole country. With their white cliffs and the sea beyond they are as important to Britain as the surrounding Alps are to the Swiss.

And then there is the climate. In a world where extremes are normal, the South Country of England offers everything that man could need to live and to prosper and to grow good things. It may not always seem like that in the bleak months of winter but, without the rain and frosts on either side of Christmas, the countryside would be neither green nor pleasant. This feeling was, perhaps, best described by Sussex poet Hilaire Belloc (1870–1953), who lies buried with members of his family at West Grinstead's Catholic church, close to his beloved Shipley, where his home was beside the windmill:

When I am living in the Midlands,
That are sodden and unkind
I light my lamp in the evening
My work is left behind;
And the great hills of the South Country
Come back into my mind
The great hills of the South Country
They stand along the sea;
And it's there walking in the high woods
That I could wish to be,
And the men that were boys when I was a boy
Walking along with me.

If I ever become a rich man,
Or if ever I grow to be old
I will build a house with deep thatch
To shelter me from the cold
And there shall the Sussex songs be sung
And the story of Sussex told
I will hold my house in the high wood
Within a walk of the sea
And the men that were boys when I was a boy
Shall sit and drink with me.

Anyone living in the South of England can relate to these words and to the tenderness which the poet feels for the county of his choice. Would that more of us deserved the following lines written by Belloc, which are inscribed on his own monument beside Shipley Mill:

He does not die that can bequeath
Some influence to the land he knows
Or dares, persistent, interwreath
Love permanent with the wild hedgerows
He does not die, but still remains
Substantiate with his darling plains!

Shipley Smock Mill

Terry Heathcote

The Old Fulling Mill over the River Itchen, Alresford

10

Along the Wayfarer's Walk

The Wayfarer's Walk stretches the seventy miles from Emsworth on the Hampshire coast to Inkpen Beacon on the Berkshire border. It is too big an area to cover properly in a short chapter, so let us concentrate on a stretch of it, watered by the upper reaches and source of the River Itchen and winding its way through and round the villages of Cheriton, Hinton Ampner, Kilmeston, Bishops Sutton and Tichbourne, all close to the old town of Alresford in the centre of the county. The Wayfarer's Walk itself, well marked and passing through some of the best of Hampshire's countryside and farmland, dates back only to 1981. Its name is a reflection of the fashionable trend to make any path or track sound as though pilgrims, highwaymen or smugglers have been passing that way for centuries; in this case, they probably have.

In the middle of March, although the weather is still brisk and blustery, daffodils and primroses, buds and birds' nests all provide hopeful signs and splashes of vivid colour after the dull, dead weeks of January and February. Crops are beginning to thrust their way sunward in the fields and grass is starting to grow in the meadows, promising better times ahead for cattle, sheep and horses, and busy ones for gardeners with lawns to mow. Nothing is certain in March, but there is the seductive prospect of good and warm weeks to come.

In addition to thousands of flowers and plants, Robin and Sue White keep some house chickens at their Blackthorn Nursery at Kilmeston, and feeding them is Sue's first job every morning. After that, it is on to the more serious task of earning a living from sowing, potting, growing, grafting, pricking out and selling all the colourful creations which the Whites get their acres to grow for them; above all perhaps, the huge variety of hellebores, which are their speciality. As they toil silently side by side in the dark, compost-scented potting shed, Robin, a stocky, balding, determined and sensitive man, well clad against a bright and cold March afternoon, has his hands deep in the soil: 'Originally we started out in this line of business when we saw an old, walled garden which was derelict offered rent free for a year in 1976. We spent eight years there slowly building up our trade and then, at last, we were able to afford to buy a piece of land here. So it was in 1984 that we moved our nursery to the top of this lovely hill in Hampshire.'

In one of his long glass-houses, Robin is working on rows of delicately coloured and petalled flowers: pinks and yellows, purples and whites, patterns and green-veined. In spite of it being early March, they are all in their full pride. 'Hellebores have always been a love and a fascination of mine, and when we first went into growing and selling them, we found, to our surprise, that they were not readily available. So we scratched around, found some sources of plants and slowly developed our own breeding strains from the ones which we bought when we first started out.'

Sue, tall, blonde, bespectacled and bright-eyed, is working with clinical speed and precision on some cuttings: 'This time of year, with spring just starting, is our busiest patch and we put a lot of hours in. Today I'm taking some cuttings of a popular herbaceous perennial. The idea is that these plants will root in a few weeks, be potted on and then make saleable plants for next spring. So, hectic though it is here now, we still have to plan at least a year ahead with what we are producing.'

Always on the move, Robin is on his way to another greenhouse to do some grafting. 'As well as hellebores, in which we hope we are experts, we grow masses of other things. We both have to do it, for financial reasons, and we want to do it. We grow lots of hardy perennials, a few, choice shrubs and, in Sue's department, a wide range of rock plants.'

11

With a razor, steady hands, sticky tape and icy concentration, Robin is cutting diagonally into a green stalk and joining it, with the a surgeon's deftness, to a more mature root. 'One of the jobs at this time of the year is grafting daphnes,' he says. 'The variety I'm working on will turn into a tall bush with deliciously fragrant flowers. It seems impossible to believe, looking at it now. But, by putting it on to a root stock which I've produced from seed, it can make a saleable plant in one season instead of three, which is how long it would take from a cutting. This is obviously a far more worthwhile way of producing a daphne bush, and the person who buys it gets just as good a plant. So everyone's happy.'

When Sue brings in a basket of intricate flowers with deep colours and twice the number of petals of the traditional hellebores, Robin takes a break from his work to rest his eyes and to explain: 'Over the last ten years, we have been developing our own strains of double hellebores. In 1971 we were lucky enough to get hold of a green-tinted double flower that had been collected in its wild form in Yugoslavia. By crossing some of our own single-form hellebores with this wild, double-form one, we've managed to produce a wide colour range of semi-double hellebores, which the people who come here to buy seem very pleased with.'

As evening approaches the Whites walk their black-and-white pointer through a copse carpeted with spring flowers beside the entrance to their nursery. Buds are starting to burst, the last of the snowdrops shine brightly, wild daffodils shake their heads in the breeze and primroses and pussy willow show off their colours as the countryside begins to awaken.

'We feel that we're lucky, being able to earn a living here in such a special part of Hampshire when so many other rural industries are struggling. We are pleased and happy with where we live and work and we both enjoy the jobs that we do. You can't ask for much more than that, can you?'

The Grey family has been farming hereabouts for three generations, since the turn of the century. The fertile Hampshire soil grows good corn crops as well as grass for sheep, dairy and beef cattle and the usual array of horses. Keeping the agricultural tradition alive, Gillian Grey Knight is one of three sisters, each of whom has taken on a share of the family acres. She specialises in sheep, but also keeps a fine bunch of cattle and some friendly house pigs. With two small children to look after as well, and a house to run, no one could describe her life as uneventful.

'When I was a child, the expectation was that girls didn't go into farming, that you did things like teaching or being a farm secretary, which is the route I chose as being the closest I could get to agriculture. But after a few years it became very clear to me that what I wanted to do was not to sit in an office and write about it, but to get out there and do it. So I took myself off to New Zealand to learn the trade and then came home and got this job on my father's land.'

Gillian is tall, slim and attractive. Her voice and manner are confident but not arrogant and she wears a jaunty waterproof stetson on her head. As she works she is watched by her two young sons. They are sitting on hay bales on a trailer and wrapped up warmly against the March gales, their pink noses peeping from above woollen scarves. A flock of some six hundred ewes is scattered across a twenty-acre windswept stubble field, the sheep gleaning what goodness they can from the ground. Gillian pours yellow streams of barley from paper sacks into metal feed troughs which are penned into a corner of the field so that the sheep cannot get at the grub until the gate is opened. A collie is in constant attendance, prowling between the feeders and giving the eye to the ewes as they queue impatiently to get at the corn. Helping Gillian is a broad-shouldered, weather-beaten man wearing only a check shirt, boots and some well-worn trousers as protection against the chill wind.

'Clive is my father's stockman and shepherd. He's a great guy and much valued. He's responsible for looking after these sheep and then, once they start lambing, he and I will work together, with extra help from a student, to get through those hectic weeks. I love every minute of it – well, almost every minute. Sometimes, in the middle of lambing when I'm up to my ears in mud, it's tipping down with rain, freezing cold and I've been up since four o'clock in the morning, maybe then I have the odd doubt. But then we deliver live lambs and everything is all right again.'

At last Clive and Gillian have finished putting out the food. They move together to the far side of the penned area, open the metal hurdles and whip back behind them as the flock charges through – scores of tons of sheep on the move. At the moment, hunger is a stronger motive than fear. Even the collie realises the wisdom of standing clear.

'This is a flock of several hundred Suffolk mules. They're due to lamb in a couple of weeks. As with all our sheep, the sire is a pedigree Suffolk ram. We feed them cake and barley daily and then they can have as much hay as they want. As you open the gate, the one thing you don't want to do with these heavy Suffolk mules is to be standing in the way, because you will be skittled. They don't want to hang around as they come in for their cake.'

And the charge is indeed ferocious. In farming, even such placid animals as sheep can, in the right circumstances, be dangerous and formidable.

Gillian's next job is special to her. She takes a bucket of sheep cake into a meadow behind her farmhouse where a small group of smart chunky ewes and lambs with the blackest of faces and the whitest of fleeces come confidently forward to meet her. 'My association with pure-bred Suffolk sheep is historical. My father bred them and my grandfather before him. And no doubt it went back beyond that too. So, once I had the chance to start farming on my own account, it was a first choice to begin breeding Suffolks again. It's only in a small way just now, but over the years I plan to build up the numbers.' There is pride in her voice and in her face as she watches the animals feed, the kind of satisfaction a mother might have as her child sits in the sun and reads a book.

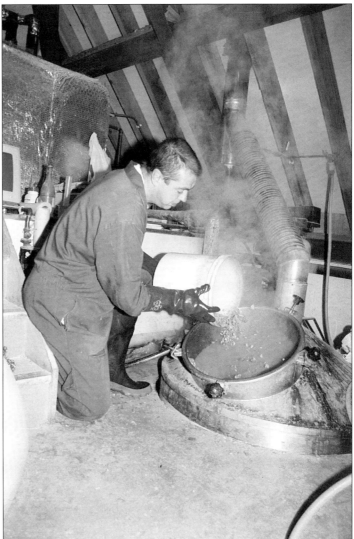

Terry Heathcote

Martin Roberts, beer brewer

The Cheriton brewhouse stands beside the Flower Pots Inn in the village. In charge is Southampton-born Martin Roberts, who has in his time worked in a dairy and as a charcoal burner. With his partner, Ray Page, he brews local beers, which are the toast of the neighbouring villages. Ale has been made in this part of the country for centuries, and today's brews are as good as anything produced in years gone by and, the locals say, a good deal better than what comes down from the big cities.

Martin is hard at work pouring heavy sacks of malted barley into a hopper at the top of the brewhouse. Gravity will carry it down to do its brewing business with the local water at ground level. 'When you're brewing beer, the main thing is the quality of the ingredients,' he says. 'Our malt comes from a traditional maltster in Castleford, North Yorkshire. Our hops come from Hereford and Worcester and the excellent water comes out of the tap.' He grins as he speaks, a big man with a ready smile, an open face and short-cropped hair.

Down below Ray is setting in motion the brewing process – opening hatches to let the barley through, turning on taps, pulling handles and releasing clouds of steam – surrounded by an array of silver pipes, drums and cauldrons. 'A few hundred years ago there were small breweries on every farm and in every village,' he tells us. 'So beer would not just have been brewed here by the headwaters of the River Itchen. It would have been produced all over the county.'

On one side of the brewhouse a giant tub of what looks like rough-grained porridge is just visible through the swirling steam. Martin explains: 'Once the grist is ready, we mash in using hot water mixed with the malted grain that comes down from above. The mash is a very critical point in the brew. You have to have just the right amount of water to the right amount of grain and it is important to keep an eye on it all the time. That, in turn, creates the wort, which is the dark, beer-coloured liquid which comes from the mash bin and goes into the copper. This brewery came into being when the landlord of the Flower Pots pub and Ray and I were sitting over a pint late one evening and chewing over the possibilities. And now it's led to all this. Great, isn't it?'

Martin is upstairs again in the wooden loft carefully tipping light-coloured hops into a steaming metal opening. The smell is scented and exotic as the warm air catches hold of the flavour of the leaves. Below, a steadily spinning rod sprays hot water on to the swelling barley grains. 'The hops, of course, are a very important ingredient. They make bitter beer bitter. They also add a lovely smell to the drink – and they even smell good before they go into it. In addition, they help to keep the beer clear. I've always thought that making beer is reasonably easy, but finding names for it is really hard. We've had some quite funny names for ours over the years. For instance, our Christmas beer is called Turkey's Revenge. And then we brewed an ale for the VE day celebrations which rejoiced in the name of Beera Lynn. We reckon our brew is one of the best pints in Hampshire, if not in the South of England. It's something we are very proud of.'

As he speaks, the dark liquid begins to flow smoothly into the fermentation tank. The smell alone is intoxicating.

Members of the Foot family from Tichborne have always been farmers, once with arable and cattle and today with outdoor pigs, which they sell on Tuesdays at Salisbury Market. They also rent out their arable land and some grazing for horses. Looking after pigs out of doors on the Hampshire clay is heavy and dirty work during the winter months but in March, with spring close at hand, things are looking brighter for Robert Foot. As he feeds and straws out his demanding herd he says, 'I suppose I started farming on and off from the time I was eight or nine years old, doing small jobs round the place. I began doing it seriously when I was fourteen or fifteen. Then I did a day-release course at Sparsholt Agricultural

Robert Foot, pig farmer

14

College near Winchester. That was every Monday and Tuesday. One day we would study livestock and the next the arable side. After that I came back home and I've been full-time here for about seven years now.'

With the help of his father, Robert is rounding up a sow and her piglets in the cluttered and old-fashioned farmyard. They use battered sheets of corrugated tin to help steer the litter towards their new sty. Several escape and scamper cheerfully among machinery and stacks of wood and metal. Bantams and chickens squawk and leap out of their path. Robert is young, lean and serious. He has deep-set eyes and a slow and steady way of expressing his thoughts, as though he has pondered each one long and hard. From the stables the heads of a couple of hunters survey the scene briefly before returning to munch their ration of hay. Robert heads for the feed store, grabs a sack of milled wheat, adds the prescribed chemicals and trudges to the paddock behind the barn, where he calls in the sows from their arks across the muddy meadow. He bangs on the stone wall to attract their attention: 'Come on, come on, feed's up.' The heavy creatures lumber forward with some difficulty over the lumpy ground. A solitary piglet trots among them, unsure what all the activity is about.

'We feed them a mixture of crushed-up corn and some minerals,' Robert explains. 'They also get additional minerals from living outside and from rooting around in the earth. That's one of the main reasons for keeping them out of doors. We also switch their main diet from wheat to barley from time to time, just to give them some variety, really. These pigs will be having their litters in a week or ten days, and we are hoping for an average of eight piglets per litter – that's the national average. Sometimes you get a lot more than that. Sometimes you get less.'

The young farmer, who in his spare time is an enthusiastic supporter of Southampton Football Club, pours a regular stream of meal out of a paper sack and into a concrete trough beside the stone building. In their haste and hunger some of the sows stumble into the feeder, so that their friends have the doubtful pleasure of enjoying their breakfast with a close-up look at some trotters at the same time. A flight of honking Canada geese swings lazily overhead in the direction of the river.

'I suppose you should compare my work to the life of those who travel to the city every day. There's far less stress and hassle with this. I start at half past seven and finish about five o'clock – a bit later perhaps in the summer when there is overtime to be done. On a farm there's always something that needs doing: fencing, hedging, repair work, that kind of thing. There's really no pressure with the various jobs, though. And you're out in the fresh air. You have this lovely countryside around you and you don't have the fumes and dust that you get in the city.'

Through the mud Robert's father drives a tractor, its foreloader piled high with straw. The son walks in front, pitchfork in hand, and shoves bundles of clean bedding into the openings of the tin arks. Inside, the young pigs leap around in excitement while their mothers munch at the empty corn ears and spread the straw out with their feet. 'We do this about once a week, whenever it's needed, really, and depending on how wet it is. For me, pigs have more character than other farm animals. You get them picking up bits of wood, carting them about and playing with them. They'll pick up the straw too, throw it around and chase it and then lay on it back-down to make it more comfortable for themselves. People have got the wrong idea about pigs. They are far more intelligent than they are often given credit for.'

Back in the farmyard the two men shift a twenty-ton load of wheat from a trailer up into the top of the granary and, from there, down into the main feed hopper. As the trailer is tipped upwards by the tractor's hydraulics, the grain slides down the smooth floorboards and streams out of a narrow hatch into a container where the hungry corkscrew of an auger carries it up and away. 'One of the jobs we have to do every month is to load up the hopper with wheat or barley, which will be ground in the mill. It ends up as the meal, which we feed to the pigs. The wheat does a good job for the sows, providing you add the right minerals to it. They do very well on it and it fattens them up nicely.' As he speaks an inquisitive head peeps out from under the gate of one of the sties. It does not seem too sure about all this talk of 'fattening up'.

Close to the woods near Tichborne Park, Brian Luff and his son Colin harvest the timber as men have been doing in these parts for centuries. The tools may be different, but the skills and traditions are the same. In the evening sunlight, a giant fallen chestnut tree is being carefully rolled over by a winch on the back of a tractor. This wood is destined for the Cheriton Sawmill, where Brian's partner, Tim Butcher, and his brother Desmond will turn it into posts, planks, pallets, trellises and anything else which their customers demand.

Tim Butcher, sawmill worker

Across the other side of the building Tim's brother Desmond is at work using another lethal saw with a six-inch-wide blade, cutting planks for pallets. 'I like working with wood because of the many things you can make out of it,' he says. 'I enjoy the different smells of all the various trees which come through this place too.'

A haughty white cockerel perches on a pile of newly cut timber and shakes its wings to get rid of the sawdust which fills the air. Tim starts assembling, nailing and stapling pallets in a sun-flecked lean-to beside the sawmill. 'Mainly we do pallets or panels for fencing and fenceposts. What anybody needs, we will do – and there's plenty of work around here. Living in the village is good too. When we were young we had no car and couldn't ever get out of the village. So that seemed a bit boring at the time and we used to say that it was a dead place. But now I'm older and I've got a motor I appreciate the village far more for what it is.'

Tim is short and stocky with a serious, rather anxious face. His hair is light brown and he is skilled with his hands. His attention never wavers from his work. He speaks with a strong Hampshire accent. As he transports half-ton logs into the sawmill on a hardworked foreloader he tells us: 'I was born and bred in the village. My father was a dairyman here for twenty-five years on the Greys' farm. I suppose he thought I was going to follow in his footsteps. But when I left school, I came up here to the woodyard – Freeman's it was in those days – and learnt the timber trade.'

It is dark and noisy inside the shed. Piles of wood chippings are underfoot. Tim eases massive logs back and forth past a vicious bandsaw which cuts thick planks with the greatest of ease: 'You've got to be very careful using this machinery,' he warns. 'I've been doing this for a quarter of a century and it comes naturally to me. But anybody new coming into the business can't just jump in at the top of the heap and expect to use the big machinery straight away. That's when accidents happen.'

The sounds of the saw and the clashing of the pallet-making drift out across the roofs and down towards the stream which runs beside the main street. Up by the church the only noise is the song of the birds.

Once a nurse, Caroline McLaughlan has lived in this part of the world since she was fifteen years old and came with her parents to live in nearby Bramdean. In addition to having horses in her meadow, she keeps bees and grows a variety of herbs in her garden. Now, using Victorian recipes, she has started to make all kinds of mustards, furniture polishes, salad dressings and potions, many of them based on beeswax, honey and herbs. To her astonishment, she has received enquiries from as far away as Japan.

Barry Miles

16

'In Bramdean, where I grew up, we had a walled-in garden. For nine years I planted and grew everlasting flowers there. I became rather tired of them and so I started off with the herbs instead. And all of this, I suppose, began from that.'

A trim handsome woman with a mobile and attractive face and dramatic grey streaks in her hair, she is efficient, purposeful and self-possessed. She wears jeans and a dark blue polka-dot blouse. Her kitchen shelves are crowded with tall and elegant bottles of her produce, each carrying a red label.

Busy at the Aga with pots and pans, beeswax, candles, turpentine and some mysterious white powder, she says: 'This furniture polish which I'm cooking up is from a recipe which was handed on by my mother. I don't know where on earth she found it. But it seems that the family has used it for years and years. It includes beeswax, candle ends, genuine turps and a magic ingredient, which I'm going to keep a secret. You melt the beeswax with the candles and then you warm up the water with the magic ingredient. At the right moment, you join the two together, stir and then cool the mixture. It emulsifies and turns into a soft and fragrant cream which soaks into your furniture. It's far better than the awful stuff you buy in supermarkets. My best customer is the rector in Cheriton, who is reviving all his pews with it as well as his front door.'

When the polish is finished and poured into its pots, Caroline moves to her kitchen table. From the window you can see oilseed rape fields stretching out towards the Hampshire skyline. The surface of the table is cluttered with bottles, bowls, pots, spoons, a sharp knife and piles of freshly picked herbs. 'I think I'll make a brand-new salad dressing today. I'm going to call it Country Ways. It will have my fennel and lemon oil in it and my elderberry and thyme vinegar. I'll also use some of my home-grown honey, some mustard and some finely chopped herbs. The honey is quite thick and solid because of all the oilseed rape around here.'

Caroline ladles honey and honey mustard into a deep bowl. The mustard she makes from seeds which she buys and mixes with the produce of her bees. She adds salt and pepper, then chopped thyme, and other herbs go into the mixture. She reaches for and pours a good helping of sweet-smelling purple

Caroline McLaughlan surveys her produce

Terry Heathcote

17

elderberry vinegar, squeezed from elderberries harvested from her garden hedge. Finally she stirs in a generous amount of lemon and fennel oil. The finished result is pink and cloudy and smells and tastes as good as a spring day looks.

In 1823 William Cobbett rode through this central part of Hampshire and wrote:

> The soil is, along this high land, a deep loam bordering on clay, red in colour and pretty full of large, rough, yellow-looking stones, very much like some of the land in Huntingdonshire; but here is a bed of chalk under this. The wheat is perfectly green in most places; but it is everywhere pretty good. I have observed all the way along that the corn is good upon the stiff, strong land. It is so here, but it is very backward.... The water in the Itchen is, they say, famed for its clearness. I now find that this has been remarked by very ancient writers.... From this beautiful spot we had to mount gradually the downs to the southward; but it is impossible to quit the vale of the Itchen without one more look back at it. To form a just estimate of its real value and that of the lands near it, it is only necessary to know that, from its source near Bishops Sutton this river has, on its two beautiful banks, in the distance of nine miles before it reaches Winchester, thirteen parish churches.

Downland at Beacon Hill, near the Wayfarer's Walk

The River Itchen, near Abbots Worthy

Terry Heathcote

20

St Swithun's church, Martyr Worthy

Near Headbourne Worthy

Terry Heathcote

22

The Worthys

Close to the north of Winchester and lying beside the River Itchen are the four Worthy villages: Headbourne Worthy, Kings Worthy, Abbots Worthy and Martyr Worthy. Here you will find some of the finest wild brown trout fishing in the South Country, the homes of rich and powerful people, and ancient churches and landmarks which have stood the test of time and of man's carelessness and folly. In early spring this is England's green and pleasant land, with lambs in the meadows, daffodils and primroses on the river banks and sticky buds beginning to show on the chestnut trees.

In 1825 William Cobbett rode this way on his much-travelled horse, recording later:

> Here, looking back at the city of Winchester and at the fine valley above and below it, and at the many smaller valleys that run down from the high ridges into that great and fertile valley, I could not help admiring the taste of the ancient kings who made this ancient city, which once covered all the hill round about and which contained ninety-two churches and chapels, a chief place of their residence. There are not many finer spots in England, and if I were to take in a circle of eight or ten miles of semi-diameter, I should say that I believe there is not one so fine. Here are hill, dell, water-meadows, woods, corn-fields, downs – and all of them very fine and very beautifully disposed.

This is notable country for fishermen and the talk in the local pubs is all of trout and flies and rods and lines. One of the centres for such things is the Rod Box at Kings Worthy, where retired gamekeeper and river minder Les Gates, Hampshire born and bred, works under the benevolent eye of his boss, Ian Hay. Whenever he can, Les is happy to escape into the great outdoors he loves so much to shoot a few clays or to fish for pike while he works on the banks of the River Itchen, one of the South's great chalk streams.

Out on a narrow meadow close to the roar of the M3 Les barks 'Pull' and two black clay pigeons sail in line abreast up and out towards the top of a leafy chestnut tree. The gun rises, steady as the hand of a great clock. A finger presses the front trigger, then slips swiftly back to the choke-barrel trigger. There are two sharp cracks and the clay discs shatter and vanish – an immaculate right and left.

Les has a tanned, countryman's face with clear, honest eyes which have in them the wisdom of the years and of the open spaces. 'I was born a keeper's son by the Mayfly at Fullerton, and my father was a water keeper as well as a gamekeeper. So I learnt both sides of the business from when I was very young. And from then on that was to be my life. I started as a keeper's boy at Handcross in Sussex in 1935 and

Courtesy Les Gates

Les Gates, river keeper

23

I came back here to the Leckford Estate in Hampshire when I was eighteen years old. I was a partridge keeper there because partridges – English ones – were the main birds they were shooting in this part of the world in those days.'

Later, wearing chest-high waders, Les stands in the swollen spring waters of the Itchen. He wields an old-fashioned, wooden-handled scythe deep beneath the surface and moves forward cautiously, swinging back and forth with a steady rhythm. Coots, ducks and moorhens call and scuttle along the margins. There are no sounds of traffic here, only the rush and gurgle of water.

'Managing the river is a bit like looking after a farmer's field. The weed grows and it has got to be kept in check. If you have too much volume of weed on the bottom it pushes the level of the water up and floods the banks. So you've got to keep the weed down to keep the river at the right height. If you have an early drought, which doesn't happen very often in this country, you don't need to do this job because there isn't the water for the weed to push up. Another thing is that, if you leave the weed uncut, it flowers in the summer and then there's a horrible mess on the surface of the water. So you've got to get rid of it. Otherwise it just chokes up and the fishermen can't cast their flies over the water, so they get no sport. As you can imagine, they're not too pleased about that.'

A heron climbs steeply and angrily away, disturbed by Les at work on what it thinks is its beat. It was hungry and was patiently trying to catch its breakfast from the river. Les, on the other hand, might be wishing that he had brought his twelve-bore with him. A swan on its nest raises its head in aggressive challenge as Les approaches its patch.

'My boss's son and I were once working the edges of the river together. We were in waders cleaning out all the muck and debris in the water. There was a big branch stuck on the weir. So I thought I'd better pull it off with a grab, get it into the shallow water and take it out of the river. I put the grab into one end of it and gave it a good heave. And I went straight in under with a mighty splash!' He chuckles, his eyes creased and narrow.

Weed floats away downstream. The river is full and powerful and promises fine fishing in the months ahead.

Both born in nearby Hampshire villages, Roy and Jean Digweed came to the Worthys in the 1950s. Here they run a smallholding, caring for their animals with much affection and patience – the main reason, perhaps, why they look in such good fettle. Roy is a dab hand with engines and machinery, which means that even old-fashioned implements can still profitably be brought into service. He points to a veteran cast-iron machine which stands waiting for work beside a clump of beet and mangels. Belt-driven by a tractor, it has done sterling service.

'That fodder-beet chopper must be pre-war,' he says, 'but it still does the job it was built for. We used to cut them up by hand with a spade. But that was too much of a good thing as well as being boring. So we advertised in a local farming magazine and we had a reply from this old boy from down Romsey way. We went down there, loaded it up and brought it back. Then I did a bit of work on it: the bearings needed greasing up, and so on. And, if I remember right, we started it up the first day we got it back – couldn't wait to make use of it. It has really saved us a lot of work.'

The chunky pink-and-white beet spill and topple their way down a trough towards the choppers and the drum. At the far end, sweet-smelling, moist segments emerge. Roy carries them off in buckets and feeds them to a yard full of contented cattle. A cock crows triumphantly. Runner ducks peck and dabble in muddy puddles. Cattle low softly and munch noisily.

'We started with just two calves and we've progressed from there. We don't much like sending our animals away, I'm afraid. They grew up here and we've got to like them and it's hard saying goodbye. We have to bring ourselves to send them off in the end, but it's not at all easy. At the moment we hang on to most of them.'

A plump guinea-fowl squawks, hops on to a wall of bales and looks down with disdain on a bunch of fifty or more Jacob sheep in a straw-filled yard. The rams boast hefty, curled horns and the rich brown and white of the fleeces is good news for knitters and sweater-makers. The flock is Jean's responsibility. 'We began with just four Jacobs,' she says, 'and they have multiplied naturally through the years. You'd be surprised how quickly you can get up to this number. I have sixty-one now. Any that are worth it we show. We've not done too well in the last couple of years, but we're hoping to have more success now.'

Jean carries heavy loads of bran and mash down to a paddock, where she pours the feed into a semi-circle of waiting troughs. When she opens the gate of the yard, a cascade of sheep – young and old, great and small – descends on the juicy mixture: 'We feed them brewers' grains from a local beer-maker and they love it. They go mad for it!' she laughs. 'You have to be careful when you feed them or they might hurt one another or even knock you flying in the rush to get at it. We bring it from the small brewery in Cheriton, and it does them just fine.'

Roy and Jean Digweed feed their Jacob sheep

She talks to the sheep as they scramble and push for their breakfast: 'Hallo, Mary,' 'How are you?' and 'Steady, girls, steady.' There is authority in her voice. 'Yes, I always talk to them. It calms them down, I think. So I say, "Good morning, girls," and they always seem to respond. One thing you can be sure of is that they will be ready for their food. I love 'em.' She sighs softly and heads back up the hill towards the buildings and the next of the day's dozen duties.

Gerald Lawrence's father was head gardener at one of the great houses in the Worthy villages. Today Gerald has the important job of helping the children of Kings Worthy primary school across dangerous roads at the beginning and end of each school day. In addition, he sometimes takes groups of the youngsters, dressed in their smart uniforms, on guided tours of the village, showing them what it was like in the distant traffic-free days when he was their age.

'It all started when one of the teachers wanted to do a history of the village. They knew that I'd been here a long time, so they asked me if I would help with it. It was a new thought to me, never having done anything like it in my life. But I went along to the classroom, talked to the children and told them what I knew about the place. And then we set out and went off round Kings Worthy so I could show them what I'd been talking about. We visited the old school – it was before this one was built.

'We go to the church, of course, right along to Headbourne Worthy and then back up Church Lane to the school. When we are in the churchyard I tell them how I was once a choir-boy and how sometimes, on the way to church or to choir practice in the evening, we used to play hide and seek in the lanes and hedges. As a result we came in late, which didn't please the music master. And we had to tiptoe into the vestry, put on our cassocks and surplices and creep up the side aisle and join in with the rest of the choir, if possible without being noticed.'

The old man, frank and friendly, with grey hair and spectacles, stands in the churchyard surrounded by an attentive group of well-behaved children. A small blonde girl in a red coat asks him if he will sing them one of the hymns which he used to sing in those days. He declines with a smile and they all laugh. They move off and he guides them on the next stage of their journey: 'Kings Worthy itself has hardly altered at all, really. It's over the other side from here, in Springvale, that the new houses have been built. That's where it's changed. The bulk of the village has moved over from here.' The handsome thatched cottages they are walking past seem to prove his point, but there is also a busy, traffic-filled road through the village, a symbol of malign change.

Eventually the crocodile of children, teachers and Gerald reaches the top of the hill above Springvale Road, where rows of new houses march across the hillside. 'In the old days, it always used to be flooded over this side, and of course there were no houses here then. Mr Key, a local farmer, used to bring children along this road in his pony and trap to school. He'd leave them at the bottom above the water and then they'd walk up the hill to school. There was hardly any traffic in those days. Anyway, with all the water there was along the bottom road, cars wouldn't have been able to make much progress down there. Things have changed so very much, just in my lifetime.' And he looks wistfully around, remembering the green hill and the water meadows as they used to be.

Terry Heathcote

Gerald Lawrence, school lollipop man and history teller

Back at the school, the children clamour for one last story before they have to go into the final class of the day. Obligingly, Gerald begins: 'In the winter of 1962 and 1963 we had some very hard weather, unusual for the south of Hampshire. The snow started to fall on Boxing Day and it never cleared up or melted until the middle of March. I can't remember another year like it. We had frost every night and the snow was six feet deep around the school. So there was a lot of cleaning up work for me to do. All the children loved it. They built snowmen and had snowball fights. They even used to throw snow at me sometimes.'

The members of his young audience exchange glances of amusement mixed with amazement. A boy flicks his arm, throwing a make-believe snowball. As the children trot off behind their friend into the school buildings the trees and bushes in the schoolyard are covered in rich, white blossom as if there had been an unseasonal blizzard.

Eve Tate is an artist who works with icing and flowers. Born in Headbourne Worthy, she used to specialise in cake decoration and in weaving delicate patterns with icing sugar and edible colouring. Today, her main work has swung over into flower arranging, although, luckily for her customers, she still keeps her hand in with her cakes and icing. Mrs Tate is often up and away at four o'clock in the morning to collect her packages of blooms from Southampton Docks. At her shop, Flowercraft by Eve, the lights seldom go out before midnight.

She is a trim, dark and softly spoken woman, her work dainty and delicate. As she speaks, she is putting the finishing touches to an exquisite pink-and-white confection of icing splendour. Her hand is as steady as a statue's.

'Quite a while ago I decided that I'd like to do something different. I had been working in agriculture for many years. So I left farming and decided to go to college to learn something new. All I had ever been able to do in this line was to rough-ice a Christmas cake. So I thought I should find out and learn how to do it properly. At first I feared that I would never be able to get to grips with it because I found it so difficult.

And, strange to say, the thing I found hardest to start with was making an icing bag. I always seemed to get it wrong and the tutor told me that I would never learn, which was not very encouraging. Anyway, after a while, I began to try things that I hadn't attempted before and I enjoyed it so much that I stuck with it as a job for more than two years. Over that time I was usually able to cope with most of the things that people asked me to do. And I still love doing it. But it's my second love nowadays, not my first, because flowers have taken over now.'

Eve handles the scissors and wire and blooms in her flower room with the same dexterity which she applies to the icing bag and the palette-knife. Rich colours and sweet smells surround her as she constructs another showcase creation for her demanding clients.

'I first started to arrange flowers when I was very young. My dad was a gardener. So I probably got my interest in them from him. When I am planning floral displays for someone's house when they have a big event like a wedding, I go and talk to them about it first. What they want is, of course, the priority. I look at their curtains and fabrics and furniture and wallpaper colours, and I try to blend the flowers with the colours and textures of their rooms and of their home. Fortunately these days we have lots and lots of beautiful and multicoloured flowers which come in from all over the world. Each job I do is surprisingly different, so I don't get bored. It's not repetitive at all, even though you're using the same materials – flowers and leaves and foliage – each time. You're never doing the same thing twice and I love the challenge of it all.'

As evening falls the lights come on in the village houses and cottages. Smoke drifts from a few chimneys. And Eve works on carefully and methodically, surrounded by vases of many colours, shiny ribbons, baskets of blossoms, bouquets and a heady mixture of perfumes.

First thing on a Monday morning, Alec Fry and his friends are hard at work in Kings Worthy churchyard, making sure that

Courtesy Eve Tate

Eve Tate, floral artist and cake decorator

it is as trim and neat and welcoming as the April weather will allow. Alec's father was a head gardener and he had his own garden plot as a child. Today, Alec's own garden in the village is a tribute to his father and to those early years of training.

And so is the immaculate state of the churchyard, where there is a bustle of hedge-clipping, weeding and whirring mowing machines. Its state is a challenge to many another country churchyard and especially to those where sheep are no longer allowed to graze safely around the gravestones, doing the good job they have done for centuries past. The ban has usually been imposed by ignorant newcomers from the towns who think it sacrilegious to have animals so close to the resting place of human beings.

'In the old days, the pilgrims on their way to Canterbury from Winchester Cathedral came through Kings Worthy churchyard. They came in through the south side and left by the north on their way along the Itchen valley. We're lucky because the people of the villages have appreciated what we have done here and have generously given us bulbs and plants and evergreens. In fact, there's one gentleman who comes from Winchester every year and brings two bags of bulbs for us to plant.'

Indeed, the spacious graveyard is ablaze with the yellow of daffodils, the purple of crocuses and the reds of early tulips. Over by the hedge some primroses peep cheerfully through the long grass.

Later, at home, Alec describes how his interest in gardening started: 'My fascination with growing things began when I was very young. We had a long garden at my childhood home, almost an acre. And we needed it to feed ourselves. Well, my mum and dad allocated a plot each at the top to my brother, my sister and myself, and they told us what we had to do and what to grow and we had to plant our own vegetables there.'

As he speaks, he is clipping the already razor-sharp edges of his front lawn, which is bordered by colourful shrubs and spring flowers in their prime. At the foot of a young fruit tree there is a splash of brightest azure from the bluebells, newly in bloom.

Alec has a soft Hampshire voice and his eyes are gentle behind his spectacles. 'My wife is the kingpin in our garden. She knows exactly what she likes and what she wants and she has organised our flower gardens and laid them out. I'm just the labourer and contented to be that. She knows all the answers with the flowers, though not so much with the vegetables. That's where I come into my own.'

While Mrs Fry carefully pricks out minute seedlings in their small greenhouse, Alec goes up to the top of the garden by the railway line and starts untying a bale of straw which has seen better days. 'We have a soft-fruit cage up the slope,' he explains. 'One of the jobs I've got to do today is to put this straw down round the strawberry plants to keep the moisture in the ground and the weeds from coming up through. When the strawberries start to arrive I shall put the runners on the top of the straw so that the fruit keeps perfectly clean.

'I like to see things kept just so. I don't like rough grass and untidiness. To have it looking like it does gives me a great thrill. And it's flattering when people stop by our front gate and have a long look at the garden and admire things. Occasionally, when I'm here, I invite them in and show them round, and it seems to give them pleasure. The other satisfying thing, of course, is when you've put the seeds in – the potatoes, the greens, the carrots and the onions – to see them all growing and getting bigger. And then you have the pleasure of going out and collecting them for a meal. I think that's wonderful and very rewarding. What more could you want?'

The place is indeed a picture of contentment. He plucks some purple sprouting for lunch, and primulas and primroses smile up at him as he works.

These Hampshire downs grow fine grass with the wet weather, though they dry out quickly enough in a drought. Above the Worthy villages, Adrian Hall and his family graze ewes and dairy cattle on the rich spring pasture. The lambs are beginning to grow strong and sturdy with the early sunshine on their backs. As the farmer climbs from a muddy Land Rover with a bag of sheep nuts over his shoulder, two collies dash ahead of him, ducking and weaving among the sheep and lambs. The scattered flock runs across the meadow towards their master. The animals call frantically to one another, the mothers temporarily uncertain whether the food or their youngsters should be given priority.

Adrian has a cheerful face and dark hair beneath a grubby tweed cap. 'On the farm at this time of the year – mid-April – we're busy with lambing. And, of course, there's always the twice-a-day milking, but then that's every day of the year, including Christmas. We're now on the second batch of ewes. We lambed two hundred and fifty of them in March and we have two hundred and fifty more about to produce any time now. We do them in two batches so that we don't choke the market or lose our sanity. So, with that and the milking, there's no let-up. In addition, we have just come through the wettest winter for sixty years or more – at least, that's what the weather experts say. We have had mud up to our eyebrows all the way through. Thankfully, we have had some sun in the last few days and it has made all the difference to the lambs. They've started skipping about and playing together for the first time this year, and that is always a good sign.'

With his swift stride he covers the ground quickly. Above the dairy stands a row of kennels with half a dozen keen-faced collies inside. When the doors are opened there are suddenly dogs everywhere, dashing about, running and jumping up the steep bank above their home, delighted to be free. In the afternoon sunshine the handsome black and white of their coats shows up well against the green of the new grass. One of Adrian's many skills and pleasures is training sheepdogs, which he also uses in his work. He goes to trials all over the South of England, though how he finds time to do it with all his other responsibilities is anyone's guess.

'When I first started shepherding, I had some dogs that weren't very good. They were unregistered and inefficient. One day I was taken to a sheepdog trial in Yorkshire by my parents-in-law. I watched the dogs working there and I couldn't believe that they were the same breed as mine. So I thought I had better get hold of something with a better pedigree and also do a bit of practising myself, because it wasn't just the dogs that were at fault. It was doing that which sparked off the whole thing, and I have been really keen on it ever since. That was about fifteen years ago. Ever since then I've had some fairly good dogs about the place.' (For 'fairly' we should read 'very', because Adrian's sheepdogs are canine experts when it comes to sheep.) 'Not all Border collies work in the same way as mine do. These have a very specific kind of breeding, which goes back a long way. There are supreme champions in their bloodline.

'There is a saying in this business that fifty per cent of any success you have is due to the breeding in the dog and fifty per cent is down to the training of the handler. But I would guess that seventy-five per cent is down to the breeding and twenty-five per cent to the handler. What you need most for training is patience. You must look at your dog a lot – straight in the eye if it's close enough – and you must try to make sure it understands what you mean, what you're saying to it and what you're trying to get it to do. You also need to give it time to develop. This is not a quick job. You must watch your dog and think hard about precisely what you're trying to train it to do. You must have no doubt at all in your mind about what you want of it.

'It's difficult for me to explain to you the fascination for me of working with these dogs. But it comes from the times when you get a collie really well trained after a lot of effort on both sides. Then it's listening to every command that you give – sometimes up to a quarter of a mile away – and responding instantly. It gives you a real buzz when you manage to get dogs working perfectly like that. It's teamwork of the highest order.'

On the top of a hill, with majestic views across the valley towards the Worthy villages and Winchester, he has set up and built a 'One Man and his Dog' course for training purposes. Huddled in a corner of the meadow six ewes look on anxiously as the shepherd and his pack of collies approach them. He selects a young dog from the group, makes sure the others are settled and secure and goes to work, standing high on a bale in the middle of the course. His voice is quiet and authoritative as he talks to the dog. There are no melodramatics. The sheep react calmly and obediently as the collie rounds them up. The dog's eyes flick constantly back to his master – he who must, at all costs, be obeyed.

The performance is superb. The sheep trot in line abreast through the final gate, which Adrian slams shut behind them. His whistles and calls (the only sounds on the hill other than birdsong) die away. He strolls over to pat the dog and to prepare the next one for the fray while the ewes rest: a contented man with his canine friends.

Much water has flowed under the bridges of the River Itchen and many new buildings have changed the four Worthy Villages since William Cobbett came riding this way in the first quarter of the last century. No doubt, if the great man returned today, he would launch one of his famous verbal broadsides at the roads, railways and housing estates which have taken away so much of Hampshire's natural beauty. No doubt, too, he would rail at the politicians, the bureaucrats, the architects and the local grandees who have allowed and encouraged it all to happen. Thankfully, however, if he could spare the time he would still be able to find that a surprising amount of riverside, farmland and village life has remained unaltered and nearly as beautiful and as innocent as it was in those quieter days one hundred and seventy years ago. Cobbett's strident voice would be a potent weapon in the battle against the malign endeavours of the high and the mighty, helping to ensure that what does remain is allowed to do so in peace from now on.

Lepe and Calshot

Terry Heathcote

Eroded cliffs, Lepe foreshore

The seaside villages of Lepe and Calshot stand guard over the Solent as it approaches the long, narrow channel of Southampton Water. Both places have witnessed the passing of thousands of great vessels through the ages, including the *Titanic*, the *Queen Elizabeth* and the *Queen Mary*, and Cape ships, tankers, containers and warships. The Hampshire coast is not, perhaps, as famous for its seaside as the neighbouring counties of Dorset and Sussex, but both Lepe and Calshot are popular with those who know about them. They bustle with waterside activity during the summer.

The name 'Lepe' is first recorded in ancient archives dating from 1277. The hamlet itself, its beach and tidy row of coastguards' cottages stand at the southern end of the New Forest and on the east bank of the Beaulieu estuary. Legend has it that there was once a causeway from here to the Isle of Wight, and this was the place where travellers had to jump across a gap in the path – hence its name. Another explanation is that the name comes from the Old English word *leap*, a basket net for catching fish. Even today, these are good fishing grounds for those who know what they are about.

Calshot, just a couple of miles away to the east, is said to have been a beachhead established over 1500 years ago by Cerdic, founder of the dynasty of the Saxon kings of Wessex. Across the waters of the Solent lies the Isle of Wight, and this is a well-known vantage point in high summer for watching the wealthy at play in their yachts and the magnificent firework display during Cowes Week. Even in the balmy months of summer, the tides and currents along these shores can be ferocious. But, with a little care and prudence, there is still plenty of seaside fun to be had in this isolated part of the southern coastline.

At Solent Sailboards by Calshot Beach, Jon Popkiss – originally from Rochester in Kent – is the boss, insofar as anybody can be in charge of those free spirits of the windsurfing world. He is a shaggy Viking of a man with smiling eyes and a ten-year-old's enthusiasm for his sport. The first sailboard was built and windsurfing was invented at Chichester Harbour in

Calshot Castle, one of a series built by Henry VIII to defend the south coast

the mid-1960s. To experts like Jon and his friends, this sport is the ultimate way of expressing themselves.

Fawley Oil Refinery stands menacingly in the background. Close at hand are Calshot Castle and the bustling Activities Centre, and across the water the Isle of Wight beckons. The shingle beach with its line of huts curves away to the north-west; if it was white sand and there were palm trees and if the temperature was twenty degrees higher you could be in the Caribbean. Jon's shop is a windsurfer's treasure trove, with hulls and masts, sails and wetsuits jostling blown-up photographs of people committing acts of heroism and insanity on their boards in twelve-foot surf. Outside Jon is using his strength to assemble his big-hulled colourful sailboard with its mighty mast and sail.

'I suppose we're all mad really. But that's the great thing about it. It's the pure essence of fun. You're so much in touch with the environment around you. It's the wind. It's the sea. It's just pure sensation. There is nothing else like it available. I had seventeen years in precision production engineering, which I loved in many ways. But when you work in a factory there comes a point when you think, Hold on – is this all there is to life? And my working environment now is simply transformed. I'm out here on the coast and, OK, it can be horrible in the winter. But I wouldn't want to swap what I have found here for anything. This is a beautiful part of England, a sensational place to sail. We can nip across to the Isle of Wight in a matter of five minutes or so. It's far, far better being by the sea than inland in the smoke. You see and hear the seabirds too. It's beautiful and I love it.'

He is at sea now, riding the waves and tugging on the boom to fill the sail, feet splayed for balance. It is blowing a force three or four in the early summer sunshine, and the spray whips off the tops of the waves as he heads out into the Solent.

'The wonderful thing about windsurfing is that virtually anyone can get into it at almost any age,' he goes on. 'We've got people down here sailing as young as seven and right up to seventy and more. And you can do it at all levels. You don't have to be brilliantly fit. You don't have to be an athlete. You can get into it at any stage in your life.' Sleek yachts pass him by as he climbs the crests. An Isle of Wight Red Funnel Ferry chugs past and, further out still, a vast oil tanker turns ponderously to make its way up to the oil refinery at Fawley.

'If you're getting into this sport for the first time, it's really important to have the right tuition, because you have to learn about the safety side of surfing, which is absolutely vital. The sea is quite a dangerous place if you treat it carelessly. You start off with a big board and a small rig. That makes it easy to get on to it when you are in the water. Most windsurfers will be pleased to help you and to show you how. We're a breed who love to help one another – and that's one of the most attractive things about the sport.'

It is later in the day. The wind has increased to force six or seven. The sky has greyed over. Across the bay at the Calshot Activities Centre, it is lunchtime and there are some major windsurfing performances in progress with boards and their pilots leaping ten to fifteen feet into the air off the waves.

Watching them, Jon says: 'You can almost set your watch on a day like this by the goings-on at the Activities Centre. During their lunch hour, when the wind is up, the instructors are always out and just blasting around over the water. We have some of the best sailors in the country there, some of the most qualified teachers. And so, the moment the wind starts blowing and they have some free time, they're out there. It's just *bang* – and they're on the water. They race around for that precious hour and then they're back inside, out of breath and happy, to show the kids how they do it. These guys are travelling at thirty-five to forty knots on occasions. And, at those sorts of speeds, if you do wipe out, it takes the breath out of you. It can really hurt. It's like hitting a block of concrete at that speed. But you rarely injure yourself. When you go down, there's a big splash. You come up with a grin, get yourself on board again, put yourself back together and go for another blast. That's what it's all about – absolutely fantastic. I'd recommend it to anyone.'

Joe Spedding, veteran fisherman

At the coastguard cottages above Lepe Beach lives Joe Spedding, one of the great veterans of the Hampshire coast. Now in his eightieth year, Joe is still one of the eagle-eyed bird wardens who watch over the nesting gulls and sea birds at nearby Needs Ore at the tip of the Beaulieu estuary. In addition, he is a sailor, fisherman, gardener and boatman, and he was an army medic from 1939 to 1945. Above all, Joe is a true man of the sea and of the countryside and knows the ways and the delights of both. He is a slight pixie of a man with a quick smile, a shock of white hair and plenty of iron in his body and in his spirit. He stands, concentrating hard, in his cluttered boathouse and workshop, weaving and winding the most intricate and complicated of fishing nets.

'End of May, beginning of June, this is the time of year when everything happens here in the Solent,' he says. 'This is a trammel net I'm working on for fishing with later this season. Its configuration is two outer sets of big mesh – one on each side – and an inner, smaller mesh. So it's like a curtain in the water and the fish hit it and make a pocket which they can't escape from. At least, they shouldn't be able to if I've done this job right. You anchor this net out at sea at night because the fish we are after move during darkness. So you moor it out there with buoys on it and well anchored down, and get Dover soles and plenty of other very nice fish.'

The late evening sun throws long shadows across the mudflats. Oystercatchers comb the surface of the shallows and fill the air with their haunting cries. Joe and his son, well booted, stride out across the mud behind the receding tide, buckets and rakes in their hands.

'The secret of successful fishing is knowing what the fish are eating. Of course, the conditions make a difference too. In dirty weather they would be feeding off the bottom for crustaceans, worms and crabs. But in gentle, quiet weather with clear water they would be hunting all the smaller sorts of fish: whitebait, smelts, that kind of thing – whatever they can find, really. And then you need, as a fisherman, to imitate what they are feeding on. And that is the real art of fishing. But none of that is a problem for us this evening, because we are after shellfish. We're off cockle-raking and that's a summer occupation. In the winter, the cockles go deep, as do many of the other shellfish – except, of course, oysters. And they come up to the top in the warmer summer months because there's lots to feed on. They eat minuscule crabs, things like that. And they're a summer delight for our tea tonight.'

The methodical collecting of cockles – each of their shells an artistic masterpiece – continues as the sun sinks slowly behind the Needles. Later, the old man sits and rests from his back-aching labours on the steep bank which leads down to the sea below his home. He is in reflective mood.

'Lepe has everything,' he says. 'It is a special place. I have been lucky enough to travel quite a bit, but this encompasses everything I like most: the sea, sailing, the fishing, water sports, free food and a living. The kids love it, the water's reasonably warm and it's comparatively safe. There aren't too many strong tides or currents. I would back it against anywhere else I've been. To me, it's home. But I would also say that it's heaven. Yes, it's a really good place.'

And there is an enthusiasm in the voice and the face – rare enough in anybody, let alone a man of eighty. Joe seems to have the sparkle and the energy of a man half his age.

It is no surprise to find horses by the sea in the New Forest. There are several places where they can reach the waterside without let or hindrance. But Calshot Beach is not one of them. Here, Stephanie Berridge, who has been running the New Forest Riding and Driving Centre on Applemore Hill for more than thirty years, transports her horses for exercise, for refreshment and for a healthy swim in the sea. It is a perfect mid-June day. The sky is blue and cloudless. Half a dozen horses and a team of smartly turned-out young riders are getting out of horse-boxes, tacking up and milling around together. Curious gulls float overhead.

Stephanie reminds her team of the importance of their hard hats as they mount and then ride gingerly down the steep, shingle bank and into the sea. 'We come here occasionally because it is superb experience for the girls who train at my stables, to get their balance right. The horses behave differently because they don't come here very often and they are not used to it. So they're excited: you can see how wide open their eyes are with the surprise of it all. And it gives them a good cardiovascular work-out too. When horses are walking normally their legs are only lifted as far as they need to be. But when they're in the sea, they have to bring their legs up and that exercises their joints. It's just like us working out in a gym.'

Stephanie Berridge exercising her horses in the sea

zon above Portsmouth as a coaster makes its way westwards.

'The thing for me about these animals is that they are such fun to be with. You can't upset them or fall out with them like you can with people. They're easy to understand. They're loyal. They're faithful. They're just so straightforward. I can relate to a horse much more easily than I can relate to a person.'

They are a good half-mile out to sea now, breasting the waves. A small grey mare is already swimming, her head and the top half of the rider's body the only things visible. A boat-load of anglers out for a day's pleasure fishing suddenly notice the horses. They stop what they are doing and watch with astonishment.

'This part of the world is lovely for us and for the horses because it's exciting,' says Stephanie. 'You've got yachts and sailboards and canoes and the ferries and all kinds of crazy things coming at you and crossing your field of vision. So it's great training for a young horse. Riding it in an indoor school and perhaps out in the Forest as well is fine. But all these strange objects don't come flying at you or floating past you in those places. I don't believe in students sitting in a class-room learning the theory of everything. You've got to get out there and do things and experience new locations. You've got to get across rivers and lakes. You must plough your way through the mud and go outside and ride in the pouring rain. When you work with horses, you get freezing cold and soak-ing wet. That's because you are out in the real world doing the real jobs. And, if you do all those things and have those experiences, you will find before long that you have a well-trained horse and a safe and reliable rider.'

As they make their way back towards the beach, battling against the weight of the water and the waves, the horses seem to bounce along in synchrony, almost like a troupe of performing animals.

They approach the sea tentatively at an oblique angle, to enter the water slowly and gently, not ploughing straight in. Early boats out in the Solent sail placidly past enjoying the sun-shine and the breeze. There is a smudge of smoke on the hori-

Treasure-hunting and metal-detecting have been the hobbies of Eric Pass from Hythe for twenty-five years. In winter or summer he can often be found scanning the beach at Lepe or at Calshot. Born in Sheffield, Eric was sent down the pits to mine coal, against his will, when he was just fourteen years old. He stood it until he was seventeen. He and his wife came south thirty four years ago and, since then, Eric has done a variety of jobs, including working on a dredger in the Solent for seven years. Now that he has retired, he can indulge his passion for beachcombing in the company of his eleven-year-old grandson, Sean.

There is still a lot of Yorkshire in Eric's voice, quick Northern humour in the expressions of his strong narrow face, and plenty of energy in his wiry limbs. 'I was at sea when this all began. It was my birthday and, when I came home off the boat, the family had bought me this metal-detector as a present. It was a great surprise to me. It was one of the very early models, one of the first to go on the market and not a patch, I suppose, on the high-tech ones of today. I had many a happy hour with it and, because it became such an enthusiasm, finished up with the posh one I've got now. It will pick up most of the iron and other metal under the sand and mud. It has found some beautiful things in its time.'

The tide is on its way out, leaving the shingle and then the beach exposed. Gulls call and circle, terns plunge vertically

Eric Pass examining his finds

into the sea after their prey, and a flight of waders skims the margin. Eric and Sean march slowly forward across the seaweed-covered shingle, moving their detectors slowly and rhythmically back and forth.

'What could be better?' asks the old man. 'Coming down to the seaside, looking for things, searching, meeting people and chatting to them – and you never know what you're going to see or what you're going to find or who you're going to meet. Marvellous, it is.'

Young Sean takes up the tale: 'We used to go to Calshot Beach for barbecues during Cowes Week – and to watch the fireworks too, of course. Grandad used to bring his metal detector, and we used to have a little look around.' This is a wonderfully polite and well-mannered boy, a credit to his family. His hair is neat and tidy and he is a keen footballer. He possesses none of the menace or arrogance of so many modern youngsters and has all the charm and interest that you could hope for.

'We used to find odds and ends together, Grandad and me. Then one day he asked me if I'd like to come to the beach with him, specially to do some detecting. I enjoyed it quite a lot, so I've kept on coming. And it's good fun.' He bends, digs in the mud with his hand and brings out a twenty-pence piece.

Eric watches with a smile. He clearly relishes the company of his grandson. 'I've been doing this for more than twenty years now. I've not found a lot in that time but, on the other hand, I did pull out a Victorian shoe patten – a kind of iron ring they used to fix to the bottom of their boots for raising their feet above the wet and the mud. That was quite exciting. I'm not sure quite how they used it, to be honest, or whether it was a lady's or a gent's. In addition to that, the other day I found what I thought was a real little beauty.'

He produces a small curved piece of metal which looks like the head of a salt spoon from a cruet. It is much stained by sea and salt. 'I've been told by some collectors that it's a Roman ear-spoon and that they used it for cleaning out their lugholes. Just fancy. It's marvellous for me because it's so old and so fascinating. I'd like to have a chance to chat to the

Terry Heathcote

36

people in Roman times about it and about their lives.' And he chuckles at the thought.

There are scores of old-fashioned beach huts along the shingle strand at Calshot. The views from them across the Solent and down Southampton Water are outstanding, and the passing ships, boats and yachts a constant entertainment. Eric and Cherry Britten from Dibden Purlieu own the property at Number Two, which has been in the family since the 1940s. For them and their children and friends, this is a little corner of paradise away from the noise and clamour of everyday life. Early on a June morning they are taking down the shutters, putting out the deckchairs and chatting to their neighbours, while a monster container ship from Malaysia steams slowly towards Southampton docks.

Eric shows us round their beach hut. 'It sleeps five people quite comfortably,' he says. 'And the best thing for us is to be able to wake up in the morning, to have our breakfast and to see the beach outside our front door and the sea just fifteen yards away. I expect you would pay a lot of money if you went abroad to be so close to the water and to the seashore. It's wonderful. You can sit together and talk and see all the boats coming and going. We saw the *Canberra* coming back from the Falklands. We watched the *Oriana* coming in when she first arrived. It's better than television. There's always something happening here on the Solent or on Southampton Water, whereas if you go to somewhere like Bournemouth and sit on the beach you hardly see anything at all out at sea.'

There is running water and a gas stove in the hut. Coffee, tea and biscuits are being loaded onto a tray. Paint is being carefully applied to a front door further down the line. Dogs and walkers wander by enjoying the fresh air and the sea breezes.

'There's a good atmosphere down here too. We get on well with all our neighbours and we all chat to one another. We call by one another's huts and look in. It's a bit like a village street, really. There's nobody stand-offish or anything like that. We're all friends.'

The kettle boils. Out at sea windsurfers battle with the waves and the currents. A Union Jack flutters from a tower poking up above the treeline. Mugs of tea and coffee are passed around. Chocolate biscuits vanish.

'People sometimes ask me, when I've been down here for a weekend swimming in the summer, whether we've been abroad, and I say, "No, we've been down to the Costa del Calshot!" And they say, "Costa del Calshot – where's that?" Because a weekend down here for us feels like a holiday. We have a big celebration here every year when it's the last night of Cowes Week. And everybody who owns a hut is here. They're all full of visitors too and guests. The barbecues are out. We have our own fireworks. And, of course, they have their big display over there at the Royal Yacht Squadron. And it's a great evening down by the water. Everyone wanders in and out of each other's huts and, if you're lucky, you get a drink when you go in. I just hope that we can keep on coming down for another few years yet.'

As the waves break softly on the shore, the Brittens settle back comfortably in their deckchairs to recover from the pressures of the coffee break. Lunch, thank heavens, is not too far away.

The Calshot Activities Centre is one of the largest of its kind in the country and is busy with people enjoying themselves all the year round. Every kind of watersport is taught and encouraged here, in addition to skiing, cycling, rock-climbing, ball games and a score of other energetic pastimes. The great wartime hangars, which once sheltered flying-boats, are today filled with hundreds of eager young people. One of the busy team running this huge adventure playground is David Gunter, originally from Birmingham, but now a converted Southerner. He stands surrounded by a group of tough-looking teenagers, kitted out warmly against unseasonal cold. They wear life-jackets and helmets and are being instructed in the use of canoes and kayaks. They look impatient with the talk and clearly want to get on with the action. When one of the instructors tells the youngsters not to panic if they capsize, they nudge one another and grin.

'These students are from Horndean Community School, which is a secondary school with a sixth form attached. These guys are part of the sixth form and they've come over to do a fairly typical course with us.' He is a tall, strong looking man. There is still a whisper of Birmingham in the way he talks. 'We were going to have some younger kids out here this afternoon, but for mid-June it's not anything like summer weather. It's blowing a northerly force six and the temperature is about five or six degrees. So, for anybody who is a beginner on any of these watersports the conditions are not particularly good. It will also be getting a bit unsafe at times. But, for experienced people like some of our instructor windsurfers, it makes for the kind of weather they relish. Because of the wind and the cold, we won't be taking even these big lads out to sea in their canoes. But we've got a purpose-built pool here which they can use for practice in reasonably controlled conditions. It's more sensible and much better for the beginners and it gives them a safe environment to work in.'

The pool is soon full of jostling canoes and flailing paddles. Some capsize with shouts of laughter. Others sway and wobble and right themselves. Some of the students are getting the hang of it. David and the instructor watch every move intently. The discipline is impressive. It might, by the look of the young people, be a problem in less able hands.

'There are two things which we at the Activities Centre think are important about an exercise like this. First, of course, there's the skill of canoeing and learning how to handle your canoe. We're also looking at how to teach them the value of co-operating with one another, how to communicate with each other and how they can challenge themselves and achieve something which they might not have thought they could ever have managed. All our instructors are skilled in both areas – the managing of the sporting activity and the right attitude to it, to life and to your friends.'

Next it is time for some competitive sport. Red canoes line up at one end of the pool and black at the other for a hard-fought game of canoe polo. The ball must be passed by hand and can only be held for three seconds. Paddles cannot be used for hitting the ball.

'These rough waters and chilly conditions make this exercise a bit more difficult for the players but they are all in wetsuits and protective gear and, in fact, it's probably warmer in the water than it is outside at the moment. Here, standing on the edge of the pool, it's about five degrees. But in it, because we've had a bit of sun recently, it's probably twelve or fourteen degrees. And, of course, the paddling and the playing keep them warm. But we won't let them suffer too much. Once they've had enough and begin to feel the cold, we'll stop the canoeing and switch to something else, probably inside one of the hangars. Because we certainly don't want to put them off or push them further than is good for them.' A goal is scored to cheers from the red canoe team.

'It's a unique location, this. And, because of the huge variety of activities we can offer and the pleasure I get from seeing the children achieve things, it's a great part of the world for me to have been lucky enough to have moved to and to have stayed in.'

Calshot and Lepe, at the southernmost tip of the county of Hampshire, seem by some magic to have escaped the worst excesses of the computer and jet ages. This is an isolated spot, except from the water, with few and narrow lanes linking the houses and hamlets. The landscape is bare and windswept. The summer views across the Solent to the Isle of Wight are spectacular. While the waves wash ashore as they have since there was a Roman port here and before, and as the trees rustle in the June breezes, the past feels very close to the present here. The poet Algernon Charles Swinburne captured some of the feelings of this seaside mood in his 'Translations from Villon' in the second half of the last century:

> I will go back to the great, sweet mother,
> Mother and lover of men, the sea,
> I will go down to her, I and no other,
> Close with her, kiss her and mix her with me.

The Watch House, Lepe foreshore

39

The view from Farley Mount

Terry Heathcote

40

Farley Mount

One of the many joys about having a job which demands that you travel through the English countryside in all the seasons of the year is that, amid all the gloom and the fears about the future of rural life, you often and quite unexpectedly come across quiet corners which seem to have remained untouched by modern ways. Turn off a busy road full of hot and impatient drivers on a July day and suddenly you find yourself in a wondrous backwater of Old England where people move at a steadier pace, think in a saner way and behave with the courtesy and consideration for which this country was once famous. Such an area surrounds Farley Mount, as far as I can discover the only hill in Hampshire bearing the proud name of 'mountain'. This Bronze Age barrow stands towards the middle of the triangle which has Winchester, Romsey and Stockbridge at its corners. On its summit is a memorial to a brave horse which, in 1733, jumped into a twenty-five-foot-deep chalk pit while out hunting and survived; the following year, rechristened Beware Chalkpit, he won the Hunters Plate on Worthy Downs.

From the top of Farley Mount you can enjoy outstanding views of the surrounding farms and woodland: north towards the Roman road which leads from the Somerset border to Winchester, and west to the valley of the River Test with its water-meadows and privileged trout fishermen. A mile to the south is the isolated church of St John at Farley Chamberlayne, one of Hampshire's finest. This exposed location might not be so welcoming in the wind and cold of winter, but in high summer, its attractions are undeniable.

The trees on the well-wooded flanks of Farley Mount are looked after by the Forestry Commission. Deep inside West Wood, Richard Baker and his team clear out the undergrowth and the unproductive saplings to make charcoal, as men have been doing for centuries in these parts. Richard, who still lives within six miles of where he was born, has in his time done most kinds of farm work but now is proud to run his own business, producing high-quality fuels for barbecues.

'Most of the timber I need for charcoal production is low-grade round wood,' he says. 'That means any sort of hardwood which has a diameter of four or five inches at chest height. These are usually trees that have been suppressed by overcrowding in the woods and need to be removed to prevent the crush becoming even worse. So I can go through the wood with permission from the Forestry Commission and do a thinning and cleaning programme for them while making my living at the same time.

'All the timber we use is from the different British hardwoods. The denser and more compact the logs are, the better is the quality of the charcoal. It's similar to when you're burning wood on an open fire at home: the harder the wood, the longer it burns.'

If he had been born in another age, Richard could have been one of the English longbowmen at Agincourt. While his metal kilns smoke and steam in the summer heat he cuts down small trees and clears away the brushwood and brambles in the surrounding thickets. He is tall, fair, strong and handsome and wields his chainsaw as if it was the weight of a chisel. Then he moves to a circular saw, belt-driven from a tractor, in a clearing in the woods. He starts cutting tree trunks into long logs; they fall on to a conveyer belt which takes them up to a growing pile beside the kilns. Meanwhile, two of his colleagues start to fill an empty kiln with the logs, arranging them in a careful, circular pattern as they work.

'Last night there was a heavy thunderstorm at about one fifteen in the morning. I was in a bit of a panic because I feared that we might not be able to get any burning done today. The trouble is that we can't unload finished kilns during wet weather – the charcoal inside doesn't take kindly to rain.

Richard Baker, charcoal maker and woodsman

As the charcoal emerges and piles up Richard fills smart paper sacks with the black chunks in a lean-to shack beside the forest track.

'It takes seven tons of timber to make one ton of charcoal,' he says. 'So if you multiply the 60,000 tons of charcoal which are imported each year into this country by seven, it gives you 420,000 tons of timber needed to make it. If you assume that there are maybe twenty tons of wood suitable for charcoal to an acre, that would make 21,000 acres of overseas forest or woodland cut down annually just to supply this country with charcoal. That's getting on for a third of the size of the New Forest. It I told the people in the South that, in order to supply their barbecue needs, I was going to cut down the New Forest over the next three years, I'm not sure how pleased they would be. In fact, they'd all be up in arms, and rightly so. But it gives you some idea of the scale of the problem when you apply it to the deforestation going on in countries around the world.'

The sun is high in the sky now. From the top of Farley Mount you can see the smoke drifting up through the trees. Richard shades his eyes with a grimy hand. 'I love working outside. I love the outdoor life. You get a good suntan for one thing and lots of fresh air and healthy exercise. But best of all it's working with nature and in the real world. The weather does not matter a lot to us. It's an unknown quantity, of course, and yes, the job is cold, wet and dirty at times. But I wouldn't change what I do for anything in the world.'

'The other problem about it is that when we load the kilns the moisture content of the wood needs to be somewhere between twenty-five and thirty per cent. If we load the kilns when the wood is wetter than that, the burning takes longer and that decreases the amount of charcoal which we get out the next day. So it's quite an exact science, really.'

The kiln is full to overflowing. The metal lid is levered and persuaded into place. With some difficulty and a few false starts, the fire is lit by a trail of paper and rags soaked in paraffin, which leads into a flue at the base of the kiln. Soon a pungent mixture of steam and smoke is pouring from the gap between the lid and the top rim of the kiln. As the logs at the bottom burn and shrink, the lid settles finally into place.

'Like a lot of farming, the charcoal season depends on the weather, not just the making of it but the selling of it as well. If you have bad weather, then obviously nobody wants to have a barbecue. So we need lots of fine, sunny days to get the punters out cooking those steaks and sausages.'

Later, watched by two playful collies, whose life in the woods is one long holiday, the men begin to unload the kiln. It has finished its job and has been cooling down overnight.

At Sparsholt, Barry Smith's vegetable garden is a source of pride and food for him during the growing months. Barry comes from a farming family, has been a farm manager and is now a plumber. When he gets home from his busy day, he is torn between his garden and his other great passion: his one hundred and fifty racing pigeons, which he sometimes takes up to the top of nearby Farley Mount for a practice run home.

'I've had pigeons all my life. I was born in Lincolnshire in the Fens. And when I was a boy, I went down onto the flatlands one day with some friends collecting birds' eggs. I don't remember if we found any eggs, but what I came home with was some young pigeons. We lived in a council house and my Dad had some chickens out the back. The chickens had their wings clipped to stop them flying away and, of course, you only clip one wing, because then, if they try to fly, they're lop-sided and can't manage it. Well, I was only seven and I didn't know about that. So I clipped both wings on my birds and, when I let them out, they flew straight back down to the Fens. Two or three days later I went back and caught them again, and I've had pigeons ever since – that's over fifty years now.'

Barry digs potatoes for his tea in the rich Hampshire loam. It is mid-afternoon and hot. He is a heavily built man, balding, with iron-grey hair, a moustache and a twinkle in his eye. A row of pigeons watches his efforts from the top of a shed at the far end of the garden. He takes the potatoes into the kitchen and soon emerges again with a bucket of wheat, which he scatters on the lawn. Pigeons plummet down from all sides to help themselves to this welcome meal.

The Plough at Sparsholt is one of those decent pubs where the landlord knows how to look after the beer, the food is good and not fussy, the service brisk and the welcome warm. Barry and a bunch of his friends are in the car park getting their birds ready for a race on the following day. The July sun shines down on them and the air is full of the buzzing of bees and the cooing of the pigeons.

'The publican is very good to us. He allows us to use a shed on his premises rent free – electricity and all – and he's interested in the birds too.' As he speaks, Barry is entering names, numbers and times into a ledger. Sweat beads his brow and drips on to the paper, smudging the ink. New arrivals come bearing baskets of fluttering pigeons.

'No one really knows one hundred per cent for sure how the pigeons find their way home. There are lots of theories about it. It's a well-known fact that they always find their way better in sunny weather. They must use the sun to a certain extent and yet, on cloudy days, they often do very well too. They get up above the cloud cover and then drop in on their target blind, as it were, straight though the clouds like a stone.'

Beside the memorial to Beware Chalkpit on the peak of Farley Mount, Barry gently lowers two baskets of excited pigeons to the ground. The birds are watchful, eager and ready to go. Away across the harvested fields lies the village and its church with Barry's house and garden close by. He opens the traps and the pigeons climb into the sky, circle twice and head for home.

'This is a good place for what we call "singling off" in pigeon racing,' he says. 'You let one go, wait a minute, then release another one – and so on and so on. It teaches them to fly on their own. Their home is only about a mile away as a bird flies and, from up here, you can see very clearly what is happening to each one when you release it. They won't have a problem because, on a fine day like this, they can see twenty-six miles.' To no one's surprise the birds are long and safely back home and waiting impatiently for their master when he returns to his house in a mere motor car.

Barry Smith with his racing pigeons

For twenty-one years donkeys have been at the centre of Wendy Andrews' life. She has nine of them and looks after them with all the care of a doting mother. But that is just the start of the story, because Wendy, third generation in her family to farm and born just across the road, also has on her smallholding near Hursley longhorn cattle, Dartmoor and Welsh sheep, rare breeds of chickens, as well as geese, ducks and ferrets. Luckily she has a husband and three sons to help her with her non-stop work.

'Donkeys are the most affectionate and placid of creatures. They look after themselves most of the time, just so long as they are fed and watered regularly and have a daily eye kept

43

on them to make sure that they are not lame or listless or unhappy.' While she talks, Wendy, slim and dark with short hair, briskly grooms and cleans another donkey and her foal, which are halter-tied to the railings of a small stockade. In the paddock geese and ducks are sharing the donkeys' water-trough – and not just for drinking. One of the youngsters kicks up his heels at the invading birds and skitters away across the bone-dry pasture.

'There's not much else to do with them other than to enjoy their company. They are certainly not a money-making con-cern. I take them out for walks or for rides with the boys and sometimes to shows, which is all pleasure, really.'

Wendy crosses the yard to take food to a bunch of fluffy golden hens which have been pecking among some straw bales in a barn. They gather fearlessly round her feet and squabble over the grain she drops for them. A young white gander dodges and weaves among them, trying to get his share of the goodies.

'I'm keen on chickens, and these Buff Orpingtons in par-ticular. They are attractive, silky birds – very tame and very quiet. As you can see, they walk all over your feet and give your toes a good peck sometimes, which isn't very comfort-able. They must think they are fat worms, I suppose.' Wendy bends down to pick up the gander, which struggles briefly and then relaxes as she feeds him corn from her hand.

'This is Giggles,' she says. 'And he's got a small problem because he's determined to believe that he's a Buff Orpington chicken. When he was hatched out, I took him home and put him with one of the chicks. Then later I tried to persuade him to go back with the geese. But he wouldn't, because he's total-ly convinced that he's a hen. I'd get him to look in a mirror but I'm afraid that it wouldn't work.' Oblivious to his prob-lem, Giggles guzzles greedily out of his mistress's hand. Perhaps he needs counselling.

The meadows slope down into a valley below the farm-yard and then steeply up again on the far side, where Wendy points out a classic grey tractor pulling an old-fashioned hay rake backwards and forwards across the grassland: 'My son Simon's Ferguson is extremely useful round the place, raking up and gleaning hay that has been left behind by the baler, carrying feed to the animals, harrowing – any odd jobs like that. They've just come in from another of our fields and, by picking up the dropped bits of hay in that way, Simon has managed to gather enough to make thirty-seven additional bales off the five acres. That's a valuable bonus because it will mean extra food for the donkeys and cows through the win-ter. So I hope we'll get a bit more unexpected hay from the meadow he's working on now.'

From across the valley the herd of heavy longhorns plods steadily up the hill, tempted by Wendy's call and by the hay she is pitching into the meadow for them. There has been a long dry spell, the grass has temporarily stopped growing, so the cattle are pleased to have these additional rations. Their mighty heads and downturned horns look like something out of Africa. The big beasts – brown, grey, black and white – snort with pleasure and nudge one another aside to get at the hay.

'I'm really keen on these animals. Their breeding goes back a long way – and they're English. I like keeping them and it's important for all sorts of reasons that the breed keeps going. They're well-behaved and quiet and easy to look after. Of course, having all these responsibilities means that we don't go away at all. But it doesn't matter because life's just one long holiday up here with the animals for me and my family, even in the wet winter months.'

Born and trained in Bavaria, Christopher Götting came to this country in 1969 and has been here ever since. Fair-haired and softly spoken, with intelligent eyes behind his spectacles, he speaks perfect English, although a trace of Germany remains. Christopher's Tamworth pigs and other animals are his hobby at his home at North Houghton, close to the River Test. His workshop is in an old granary a couple of miles to the south-west of Farley Mount. Here he designs, crafts and con-structs violins of the highest quality for some of the world's great musicians.

He feeds his vast marmalade-coloured pig and her litter stale bread before he leaves for work in the morning: 'The largest pig is a pedigree Tamworth sow. She's called Fergy, not so much because of her size, but because of the colour of her hair, which is golden red. She's been with us for five years now and she gives us a fine litter every year. They are good pigs – quiet and easy to look after, a rare breed and we are pleased to help keep them going.'

The barn where Christopher works is light, spacious and airy, with sun-streaked wooden floors. It is perched on staddle stones, originally intended to keep rats and mice away from the stored grain, and has a secure, grey-tiled roof. Inside everything is neat and tidy. The smell of wood, paint and varnish pervades. A golden labrador lies asleep in the sunlit doorway.

'After many years working in London and restoring violins – many of them very old and precious ones – I decided that I wanted to set up on my own and make new instruments. Of course, it was very useful and helpful for me to have spent that time doing the restoration work because you can learn so much from the old masters and the way they did things. So I try to use the knowledge and insight which I gained from them when I start work on a new violin now.'

As he talks, Christopher is gingerly shaping the wooden handle of a violin with the sharpest of sharp knives and the most detailed, minute measurements. Everything he does is painstaking and unhurried. The smallest discrepancy in dimension can make all the difference to the sound of the instrument.

'From very early on in my life I wanted to do craft work with my hands. It's a desire that always existed inside my head, I guess. I had the great opportunity to work with a violin-maker in my home town in Germany in my youth. After that experience, I decided to go to a violin-making school in Bavaria, which is still there today. So that's how I started down this road.'

Upstairs in the barn's loft, exquisitely shaped violins hang from the beams. Sunlight gleams and reflects from their seductive curves. At his workbench, bent over a pestle and mortar, Christopher is crushing, mixing and pounding and adding liquid to the ingredients of the precious varnish with which he stains and colours the surface of his instruments. In

Christopher Götting, violin maker

the mixture there is every shade of pink, brown and rose.

'This varnish is important to the violins for a whole number of reasons. It makes them look beautiful, of course, but

45

there's far more to it than that. It's naturally important that they look good. They are, after all, for the purpose of entertainment. And it's interesting that, if you compare the look of the old instruments with new ones, the veterans are often superior. Another value is that varnish is vital for the sound of the violin. If you apply the wrong substance to a well-made instrument, it won't age well and the sound it produces will deteriorate over a period of time. It takes me about two and a half months to make a violin. I try to work with traditional methods and to use machinery seldom. I attempt to achieve the style of Stradivarius and the other great craftsmen of the past. But I never make specific copies of individual antique instruments.'

On the steps of the barn Christopher sits quietly in his lunch-break and plays softly on one of his new instruments. His eyes are far away. His dog lies sleeping at his feet. 'I love living out here in the green countryside,' he says, 'and I am lucky indeed to have this rustic workshop, where I can concentrate on my craft and can get some inspiration from my surroundings as well.'

Rob Hugg and his friend Geoff Piper are window cleaners in the pretty villages which surround Farley Mount. It is an idyllic job in the summer months with the gardens in full bloom, though not so much fun in January and February, perhaps. In his spare time, Rob – sometimes with Geoff's help – builds, paints and restores gypsy caravans. It is in this work that Rob's heart and head are mainly engaged.

'When I was eleven my mother and I went to Reading to the cart and trap sales to look at gypsy caravans. My love for these wonderful vehicles started then and has grown ever since. Later there were a couple of gypsy chaps who lived in the New Forest and who used to make some of their money painting carts and carriages and caravans. They said that they'd teach me what they knew but that they couldn't pay me. And I was with them for six months to a year, I sup-

Rob Hugg, gypsy caravan restorer

pose; learnt a lot from them and then started doing it on my own. And I still enjoy it today as much as ever I did then.'

The barn is a treasure trove of old horse-drawn vehicles with rich colours, curved shapes and traditional patterns. While Geoff paints the head of a shaggy piebald cob inside an oval frame on the side of a veteran ship of the road, Rob is using a long feather brush to make sweeping swirls and curves on a dark green caravan alongside. Both men work with the utmost care and concentration, surrounded by the clutter of their workshop and the smell of paint, freshly cut timber and glue. Outside in the fields the combines and balers are hard at work as the harvest begins to come in.

'When I first came up here and started doing this work, Geoff would come along and he'd see my horse heads and would say that they looked like pandas. So I said to him, "OK then, you paint them." So he did, and all my customers, when they see Geoff's horses' heads, they think they are transfers because they are so good and so lifelike. So now I leave them to Geoff and I get on with all the other stuff.'

He moves over to a workbench at the back of the barn, squeezes some wood into a vice and starts shaping it with a chisel, which cuts the wood as easily as if it was putty.

'A lot of the skills I have had to teach myself. It has meant many hours of practice. I used to spend days at home in the kitchen with pieces of wood and my lining brushes doing those difficult scroll linings. In those early days they looked awful and it makes you depressed because you think you are never going to master it. Then eventually you do one which looks like what you're trying to achieve and that's like some kind of miracle. Of course, you never stop learning and you go round and look at hundred-year-old gypsy paintwork to see how the old boys did it and polish up your skills and your ideas that way.'

A heavy piece of hand-driven metal machinery stands in a corner. It looks as though it might have come out of the ark.

46

The two men approach it and start working on the spokes of a cartwheel, preparing them to fit into the rim, which is standing ready.

'This is our tongue-cutting machine,' Rob explains. 'It's a very old bit of gear and it's original. It's sometimes a bit temperamental and it doesn't always cut the tongues quite as neatly as you would like. But it's lovely to be using something that the old boys would have been working with sixty or seventy or eighty years ago and more. And, when it operates as it's meant to, it's a really good machine. Because I like operating it, I cut all the tongues on my wheel-spokes with it.'

With Geoff's help he pushes a spick and span green-and-yellow caravan along a lane to the shed where it will be housed until its new owner comes to collect it. In the summer fields a straw-baler passes by, pushing straw packages out of its maw.

Watching it, he says: 'There's a romantic gypsy notion which I share about life on the open road and travelling around without too many definite aims beyond survival. It's an attractive way of life, hard at times, but always accompanied by the sound of horses' hooves on the gravel or the tarmac, and the iron wheels rumbling along. It's almost musical and a great improvement on the rat race.'

It is a July morning and harvest time at South Lynch Farm, Hursley, near the western edge of Winchester, and Andy Bull, whose family goes back for many generations in the area, has been cutting the barley with his giant green combine harvester since the dew was off the crop. After six years in the RAF, Andy became a self-employed farm worker and relief milker. But now, after training for two years, he has become a fully qualified cattle chiropodist and foot trimmer. One of only fifteen in the country, he gets calls from as far afield as Suffolk and Devon.

'I used to love driving tractors and combines and I used to hate working with cattle,' he says. 'I never took on a job with them unless I absolutely had to. But as I've grown older I've begun to do less of the arable side and I've started to feel much keener on the cattle side of things. I still do the driving, of course, and for two months of the year you'll find me back sitting on a tractor or a combine and passing the summer away in the cornfields, because it's good work during the warm months. The weather is usually kind, the views are pretty up here and it's a pleasant change for me to work with people, because the other ten months of the year I'm usually on my own – apart from the cows, that is.'

Andy is young, quick and vigorous, with short black hair and an easy smile. He stands beside a metal crush as a large Friesian cow is helped slightly unwillingly into it. The metal cage will help keep the animal steady and secure while Andy works on her feet.

'I was milking the cows on a farm not far from here and a foot-trimmer turned up there one day. I helped him get the cows ready and watched him working on them, and the job he was doing looked interesting and appealed to me. So I made a few enquiries about how I might get into that kind of work and, before I knew it, I was whisked off to Holland, where I studied cattle chiropody for two years as well as the techniques for trimming cows' hooves.'

The cow is calm in the crush. Andy has protective gear on his arms and his legs. The cow's weight can do considerable damage if it jams you up against a rail. A queue of fine black-and-white cattle looks anxiously on, each one hoping that it is not her turn next. Andy is operating a sling with a ratchet winch which allows him to lever the cow's rear leg up into a position where he can work on the hoof. But he is uncomfortably close to the creature's back end.

'In the olden days the herdsman would trim the hooves himself as a regular part of his job. But in those times the diet that you fed the animals was not like the food you give them nowadays. There's a lot more proteins, a lot more minerals and vitamins going into the cows today to make them produce as much milk as possible. As a result of this rich food the horns and the hooves grow faster than ever they did before. It's this problem in particular that produces a lot of growth in the cattle's feet.'

After cleaning the muck and mud off the hoof with a metal

scraper, Andy carves, shapes and trims the outside of the hoof with a razor-sharp knife. Wedges of the material fall to the ground. He is removing what looks like an alarming amount. The cow has come to terms with her ungainly position and stands there placidly enough, slowly chewing the cud and exhaling grassy gasps of breath. She shows no sign of pain.

'What I am aiming to do is to produce a weight-bearing difference on the inner claws of the cows' back hooves and on the outer claws of their front feet. The reason for doing this foot-trimming is that a cow with bad or unbalanced feet will only be able to get around the meadow to eat enough food to produce the goodness to keep her going and alive and not enough to produce much milk. So bad feet mean less milk and less money for the farmer.'

The owner of the cows, a tall, serious-looking man with a moustache and a face that looks accustomed to confronting problems, stands at the animal's head and watches on with concern as Andy works his magic.

'It's amusing as you go round from farm to farm doing this job. You meet lots of interesting people and you single out quite a number of individual cows too. Some of them you always remember. Number 63 springs to mind. She was on a farm in Wiltshire. She used to go round biting the other cows and, when you were working on her front feet, she used to nip you in the middle of your back. Those are the sort that stick in your mind all right.'

The beast's leg is gently lowered back into its normal position and, with a shake of her head, she ambles back to join her friends in the field. Andy prepares his next patient. The dexterity and speed with which he does his most delicate job are remarkable.

'They are not unlike human beings in some ways. You get ones that seem to have better developed characters than others. You come across some that always kick out at you and you also, unfortunately, get the ones that will always cover you in muck. Come to think of it, it's not a clean job being stuck behind the back end of a cow all day. My wife gets

Between Farley Mount and King's Somborne

cheesed off when I bring her home several sets of dung-covered overalls to wash. But in the main it's satisfying work which brings in the money to pay the bills as they arrive, and I enjoy doing it.'

They say that poetry is a universal language, applicable to all sorts and conditions of people and places. In *A Shropshire Lad*, written in 1896, A.E. Housman describes scenes and feelings which his twin in this part of Hampshire might well have echoed:

> Into my heart an air that kills
> From yon far country blows
> What are those blue, remembered hills
> What spires, what farms are those?
>
> That is the land of lost content
> I see its shining plain
> The happy highways where I went
> And cannot come again.

The Watercress Line

The Watercress Steam Railway Line crosses the centre of Hampshire between Alresford and Alton and runs parallel to and to the north of the A31. Its locomotives have been steaming back and forth for more than twenty years, though there has been a railway here since 1865. So the present system is far younger than the engines themselves and a mere toddler compared to the flourishing cress beds from which it takes its name and which have existed in this fertile part of the county since early this century. The River Itchen rises up here beside Ropley Dean and flows south towards Southampton and the sea. It is a famous chalk stream, beloved of skilled wild brown trout fishermen. It also provides much-needed water for farmers and villagers and, as rivers always do, brings serenity, wildlife and green water - meadows to the countryside.

Although Basingstoke, Winchester and Aldershot are close at hand, this can still claim to be a pocket of true rural Hampshire, with its woodland, productive farmland and pleasing landscape. Hidden away deep in the woods over Bramdean Common is a little tin church built specially for the gypsies who once came and camped here in their hundreds. And Alresford – 'the ford by the alders' – has a distinguished history of cricket, sheep farming and flour milling going back over the centuries.

September is a grand month for coming to this cultivated part of Hampshire, when the harsh heat of summer is behind you and the chill of autumn still a few weeks away. Meanwhile, local people get on with the routine of their everyday country lives, much as their forefathers have done for generations.

Bicycling is probably the sanest way to travel these narrow Hampshire lanes and, for Henry and Doreen Goode from

The church in the wood at Bramdean

Terry Heathcote

Holly Lodge at Ropley, it is also the most pleasurable. Henry's father was a carter who worked with heavy horses, earning two pounds ten shillings a week with a pint of milk as his perk. Doreen is the daughter of a market gardener from just up the hill above the village. The three-acre smallholding where they have lived for forty years, and where they grow most of what they eat, was bought for twenty pounds just after the First World War.

The couple might well have been transported from the last century, to judge from their appearance and their attitudes. Henry is tall, thin and wiry, with a battered hat on his head and a ready smile below penetrating, thoughtful eyes. Doreen was surely an English rose in her time, with fair hair and healthy good looks. While she mows the grass with a veteran machine, Henry is busy cultivating one of their substantial vegetable patches: 'We've always grown all our own vegetables, because it helps out financially and we don't much like the vegetables that you buy, as almost all the farming today is chemical farming and not organic. We've found our home-grown produce is as good as anything in the shops. We have some failures, but mainly we grow and harvest some good stuff.' And he smacks his lips with satisfaction.

Doreen, meanwhile, has finished cutting the grass and is carefully collecting seed pods from a creeper in the hedge. 'I learnt most of my gardening tips from my father,' she says.'With him being a market gardener, we always had to be helping out from when we were very young. It was a busy life and a busy childhood with all the cutting, weeding, growing, harvesting, pricking out seedlings and so on from springtime right on through the year. And I think those times have given me a lot of my values today – coping with nature, collecting seeds and planting them, dealing with real life. I love all the flowers and vegetables, even those I haven't heard of! But I'm afraid I still go for the old ones, which look so lovely and traditional. I suppose I'm just old-fashioned.'

Henry is clipping one of the high garden hedges with some venerable shears – no electric cutters for him, sensible man. His voice and accent come from years of Hampshire living: 'I've always been interested in nature and I've always been interested in man and his life. When you take notice of how the world is going along – its past, its present and its future – it does seem that the cleverer man becomes scientifically, intellectually and academically, the weaker he becomes mentally, morally and physically as well. It may seem like a contradiction but it appears to be true.'

There are ducks, geese, bantams and chickens all over the place at Holly Lodge. Their cries and clucking are a constant reminder of their presence. Doreen's job in the morning is to check their water and food troughs and to feed them some grain as a treat: 'My bantams are good to have around, like the rest of 'em. And then you've got lovely fresh eggs with golden yolks. They're only fed good things and it means we're self-supporting in that area as well. And the result is that my cakes and sponges are so much tastier too. Everyone who comes here seems to like them – children, grandchildren, friends. It's satisfying for me. I'm always cooking up things with those eggs.'

High on the top of the bungalow, Henry, perilously perched on a wobbling ladder, is giving the roof a thick coat of bright red paint. 'The roof is made of corrugated iron – there are several like this hereabouts – and I have to paint it every five or six years,' he explains. 'Between times I need to keep an eye on it. It just depends how it wears because, of course, some paints last longer than others. And the last thing in the world I want is for the metal to get rusty. Years ago for this job people up here would use red oxide paint on their roofs. That used to make a good job of keeping the rust away, you see. But I use gloss because I get a better shine out of it. It looks better, I think, so it makes the work more rewarding to do.'

He turns back to his task. There is no rush or hurry with the Goodes. Each job is one that needs doing in its allotted time. It will be done painstakingly and properly. Boredom does not seem to enter into their calculations in their country idyll.

It is now late afternoon and, having come down from the roof, Henry is in one of the paddocks adjusting some bolts in the engine of a red tractor. It is in mint condition, although it must be fifty years old. Doreen passes by and pauses for a chat. She has a bucket in her hand. A white and woolly pony surveys her and what she is carrying with interest. 'He's called Frisky,' she says. 'Not a particularly suitable name nowadays because he's over thirty years old. He's just a pet – we do have one or two of them as well as the animals that have to earn their keep – and the children and the grandchildren love him and ride him and spoil him. There's not so much riding for them now, I'm afraid, just a little from time to time, because he's getting on a bit. But he's a tough old boy and, as long as he keeps on eating as he is at the moment, I think he'll soldier on for a while yet.'

Frisky's nose is deep in his bucket. A cat yawns and stretches in the sun. There is peace and contentment here. The Goodes live up to their name. Country people to the core, they are part of a breed that is, alas, vanishing in their care, their responsibility and their unwhining, thoughtful acceptance of life as it is and as it should be.

The Watercress Steam Railway Line is a feature of this part of central Hampshire. Once part of the national rail network and founded over one hundred and thirty years ago, it is today mainly a tourist attraction, enthusiastically run and cared for by volunteers from all over the area. One of them is Arthur Blake from Andover, who after spending forty years as a bus inspector enjoys working as a porter at Ropley Station. Old fashioned it may be at the station, and deliberately so, but it

Full steam ahead on the Watercress Line

Eric R. Langley

is also busy. Trains shunt and rumble. There is all the hurly-burly that goes with transport, coal, water and big engines. And everywhere are the unforgettable smells and sounds of steam.

The scene takes you back to the 1940s and 1950s, to the days of rationing, bombed-out buildings and *Brief Encounter*. Shrill whistles sound and echo. Over the tannoy Arthur's clear and precise voice intones, 'Ropley, Ropley'. There is the sound of escaping steam, grinding brakes and wheels, coal being urgently shovelled and the roar of the furnace. The bewildered and excited face of a six-year-old girl in a pink jumper peers out from one of the carriage windows as the train pulls out of the station.

'Although I hadn't been here, I had read about the attempts to keep the railway going in the local paper,' Arthur says, 'and one day I came over and found myself sitting and watching a train coming in with the engine pulling it, steam pouring from the smoke-stack. For some reason it made me think of one of those beautifully designed sewing machines – worth hanging on to. And I began to wonder how on earth they dreamt it all up and what each piece of mechanism was for. It's complicated all right. It's geometrical, but it's a work of art to me.

'People sometimes say to me: "I went to school on this railway when I was a child." It meant something to them. At the time, they probably thought nothing of it, but now it's important to them. Steam in itself is fascinating because, if you let a little steam into a pot and leave it, it will expand and provide strength and energy for you. And it does it so quietly, leaving out the chuff-chuff of the exhaust. But the steam action itself is positive and deliberate and it's under man's control. It's real power and it's being created there on the spot in the loco-motive. It's quite extraordinary if you allow yourself to think about it.'

Sharp of eye and slim of frame, Arthur sees another train off to Alton. It slides past him as he stands watching on the platform. Rain begins to fall.

'We have some pretty hard days up here, quite strenuous work. And I know that all of us go home feeling a bit

Eric R. Langley

Arthur Blake, volunteer porter on the Watercress Line

'When I was five years old I went on a long holiday to stay with some relatives in London and, as no one could go with me at the time, I was put into the care of the guard as a sort of live parcel on his steam train. I was met at Waterloo, of course. And, ever since then, I always enjoyed riding on these trains as a youngster or standing on a bridge over the line and watching them go underneath and being wrapped from both sides in a blanket of steam. I used to enjoy it very much – the clickety-click of the wheels, the sound of the whistle and the roar as you went into a tunnel. I would hardly ever sit. I would stand in the corridors watching the telephone wires dip up and down as we went by, and I would find myself humming a tune of my own making to the sounds of the train as we went along in time to the dip of the wires or the click of the wheels or both.'

The train speeds on its way through the matchless Hampshire farmland. The furnace is crimson. The driver looks forward out of the cab window, the wind caressing his hair. This is civilised travelling of a kind which most of the world has forgotten and which calms rather than shatters the human spirit. The hideous hell of the motorways seems a million miles away.

The watercress beds hereabouts, beside many of which the steam railway runs, date back to the 1920s. For a hundred years and more the cress was grown and gathered in ponds and ditches. Because of the purity of the water from its artesian wells deep in the chalk, Hampshire has a well-deserved reputation for the high quality of its watercress. Mervyn Smith, the son of a charcoal burner, started on the beds at Bishops Sutton when he was fifteen and has stayed with the crop ever since. He is a sturdy bespectacled man, tanned by constant exposure to sun, wind and rain. His concentration as he harvests his rich, vivid green crop is absolute.

'Learning to cut cress properly takes a couple of years,' he says. 'It may look easy, but it isn't, I can assure you. You end up cutting your fingers a lot to start with. And you have to have a very sharp knife. The only way to learn is to do it, like so many

whacked. But, however tired you may be, there's always the satisfaction of knowing the job is well worth doing.'

The train from Alton, bound for Alresford, pulls into Ropley Station. The driver hooks with his arm the station purse held out to him by Arthur as the cab passes by. Arthur walks along the platform to beg some coal from the fireman to keep the waiting-room stove warm for the passengers. Then he takes up his story again:

other jobs, and to improve as you go along and get experience.'

Mervyn nonchalantly trims the base of a huge fistful of cress as he strides and splashes through the waterbeds, the blade missing his fingers by millimetres.

'Normally this time of year, September, when we've cut a crop of cress, it takes about five or six weeks to grow back up again. Then, when it's ready, we're out early as usual to cut it once more and send it off to market.'

His next job, in the neighbouring bed, is to roll an immaculate swathe of rich green growth with an ancient slabbed wooden roller, pushing it back and forth while the water gurgles beneath. The instrument creaks and groans with a regular rhythm.

'The reason I roll the cress soon before harvesting it is that it helps if it's pressed down to come back up at a bit of an angle to make it easier to cut. In the winter months I also have to roll it regularly to help protect it from the frost. The water temperature is always warmer than the air temperature.'

Behind it the roller leaves straight rows of light and shade, as at Wembley Stadium or at Wimbledon, as Mervyn squelches backwards and forwards, pushing it along with his strong arms and the weight of his body. This is no job for weaklings.

In the chill brick packing-house the only sound is of constantly running water. Local women bunch the cress, which the boss has brought there in crates, and pack them tidily into white crates. Crushed ice is piled on top in abundance before the lids are fastened on. Underneath the dripping table, a lad of five or six years old, his thumb firmly in his mouth, looks out anxiously at the adult world.

Mervyn Smith, watercress grower

'The business has changed a lot in my working lifetime. When I started out it was seasonal, far more than it is now. We used to stop in June and then start back up again in October.

Now it's an all-year-round season, no let-up at all. The cress we're packing today is going up to Covent Garden, Western International Market and Brighton and Southampton markets. We sell some locally, including at the nearby farm shop and, I'm proud to say, none to any supermarkets.'

Water bubbles up busily from the top of the artesian well beside the kiosk where farm produce of every kind is on sale. Customers come and go to buy fruit and vegetables. There is a hand-written recipe for watercress soup pinned to the door.

Beside her farmhouse on the old gypsy common at Bramdean, Caroline Rose-Silk, wife of an arable farmer, breeds and keeps miniature horses. Originally from Pembury, near Tunbridge Wells in Kent, Caroline has lived here for twenty-five years. Once she kept rare hens and bantams, but today it is these unbelievably small horses which have taken over her time and her energy. Guinea-fowl and a couple of bantams peck at the grass on the common as a pint-sized pony and trap approach with Caroline at the reins and a grandson beside her. The handsome piebald pony looks quite pleased with himself.

Caroline explains: 'A lot of people have them simply as pets, because there is not a lot you can use them for other than driving them. When we started out we went up to the Reading carriage sales and we bought a tiny breaking-in trap. Having got that, we broke one of the horses to harness this summer. It didn't take long and, so far, he seems to be very good. As far as I can tell, he enjoys it and it's good fun for us too.'

A cheerful springer spaniel trots along beside the trap. As they cross the common some of the longer clumps of grass are higher than the pony's ears, which bob and peep above the grass-heads.

Terry Heathcote

'What I'd like to do is to drive a team of four of them. I've seen a picture of one, though I've never seen one in the flesh. Because they're so small, children aren't frightened of them and it gives them confidence when they first start with ponies or horses.'

Later, Caroline walks across the grassland with a gaggle of children and grandchildren. They are taking three more of the miniature horses for a walk on leads as though they were dogs – and not the biggest of dogs, at that.

'A normal-sized pony is rather big and awe-inspiring to children of this size and age. They're only about four years old. So I think they feel happier with these little chaps. They haven't been hurt or kicked yet and let's hope they're not.' As she speaks a blond lad tugging his pony along behind him runs ahead across the common. He seems unperturbed by the little black beast bucking and shying behind him like an animated kite.

'There are some people in the breed society we met last year who have two or three of these horses as well as three large dogs. They lead them all up into a horsebox – dogs and ponies together – and take them to a nearby field. They open up the back and let them out and they all run around and play together as though they were the same creatures. When they've had enough exercise, they call them all in and they clamber back into the box together and home they go. It's unusual, to say the least.'

Her two miniature stallions are up on their hind legs and exchanging blows, joined together like boxers in a clinch. Their high-pitched whinnying and aggressive snorts startle a flock of pigeons, which fly across the evening sky, wheeling in towards their roosting place in the wood on the far side of the meadow.

David Terrill and his son Philip have had distinguished careers managing one of the great Hampshire estates. With that invaluable experience behind them, they have now struck out on their own on five hundred acres of rented and bought land, most of it in the Itchen Valley. They breed Hereford cattle and grow corn and grass. David also has a successful vegetable garden. And now, as an experiment, he is working on the idea of breeding and producing worms for fishermen.

It is first thing in the morning on their farm. The sun is up and a warm September day is in prospect. Philip drives his tractor sedately up the yard towards a grass meadow. In a cage on the back are two Hereford calves, tottering uneasily with the movement of the machine. They are closely followed by their anxious mothers.

'My family has worked with Herefords in this part of Hampshire for well over fifty years now,' he says. 'And I believe that these magnificent red-and-white beasts have still got a great part to play in converting grass into beef economically and without having to feed them lots of concentrates.' The farmer slowly releases the calves from their temporary prison and they trot off cheerfully behind their mothers over the lush green pasture. The deep red colouring of the cows is set off dramatically by their white patches.

'I've got a soft spot for Herefords and, contrary to what everyone else seems to think, I don't want any continental breeds. These are the first two of our autumn calvers – one was born last Friday and one on Monday – so they're both less than a week old. This is their first time out in the field. The mothers will have a good bit of grass out here and produce plenty of milk, so the young 'uns will get a good start in life. They'll stop outside together with their mothers for six months and have a jolly good time and grow fast and well.'

Out in the sunlit yard David Terrill is putting a twenty-ton trailer of wheat through the mobile corn cleaner and drier. As he releases the metal hatch a golden stream of corn pours down into a complicated series of augers which carry the grain up into the drier. Dust pours out of the machinery into the still air.

'This is the last load this year of our harvested corn. I've measured the moisture in it and it's reading seventeen per cent. Well, for safe storage and for sale it needs to come down to fifteen per cent or below. So perhaps we can take advantage of the sunshine today. That will help the drying process enormously, and we're very much hoping that we can bring it down swiftly to a safe moisture level.' The old man, with his strong, aquiline face and stubborn jaw, screws his eyes up

Philip Terrill with a fine Hereford calf

against the sun and the dust as his precious crop tumbles and turns through the tall drying drum.

Next David heads for a dark shed beside the farmhouse, where his latest enterprise is housed. This is his first crop of earthworms – thousands of them – with their shiny eggs and minute offspring struggling and twisting in the black soil.

'This is the start of the life cycle of the worms. The yellow eggs are correctly called cocoons and the tiny worms are recently hatched. To some people this may seem to be a stupid, old man's idea. But there does seem to be a demand for worms for fishermen. It's something that I've studied and looked at over the last few years. There's also a need for them in sewage works to break down the sewage and on land reclamation sites. I'm told that Ireland imported five hundred tons of worms last year for that purpose. So I think that there could be a sale there too. The other virtue of them is that the final material which the worms produce is valuable.'

David picks up and runs through his hands the black crumbling compost. 'This started life as farmyard manure and vegetable waste. Then we put the worms in it and it's now top-quality field fertiliser. It's completely friable, and

even as we speak, Philip is out spreading it on one of the pastures to see how the grass will respond to it.'

The Hereford cattle look across the fence in shocked disbelief as the dung spreader flings the manure out on to what they had thought was next week's provisions. In a month or two they will reap the benefit.

Whatever the controversy it arouses and in spite of the strong feelings on both sides of the argument, in September the fox-hunting season is getting into its stride and hounds and horses and men are preparing for the hard months ahead. Bob Collins is the huntsman for the Hampshire Hunt and, early on a Tuesday morning at his Ropley kennels, he and his colleagues Adrian Smith and Michael Murphy are preparing to set out for some much-needed exercise.

Son of a Somerset dairy farmer, Bob has been working with hounds for more than twenty years: 'I worked back home on my father's farm for twelve years milking cows. I didn't like it too much because I thought I should be out hunting. I used to hate having to come home early on hunting days – my Dad made me get back in time for the afternoon milking, and I decided then that, if I wasn't happy doing that job, I'd be better off leaving and trying to do something like this. And I've never once regretted it for a moment.'

Bob is a hefty, tough man with traces of Somerset still in his deep voice. As he talks, his pack of hounds look out eagerly from behind the bars in front of the kennels. There is much baying and scrabbling of paws against the metal gate. Soon the men in pink coats and hard black hats are here, mounted on glossy and mighty steeds. With a *rootety-toot* on the hunting horn, the crack of long whips and shouts of encouragement, hounds, horses and men stream away across green, sunlit meadows, along narrow lanes with high hedges and through centuries-old woodland.

'Hounds become part of your life. You get attached to them like friends,' says Bob. 'Each one has its own name. They all have their individual characters and they're just wonderful to be with. You do have to train them to a certain extent, though most of what they do is instinctive. But with the roads so busy now, we couple the puppies to older hounds to teach them how to behave and what the dangers are. That lasts about three weeks and teaches them not to go over the white lines and general roadside discipline. One of our rules is that they are never allowed to cross a line in the road – and they obey.'

It is a sight as old as history and the noises are just as evocative: the distant sound of the horn, the echoing hoofbeats and the occasional yelp or call from the pack: 'We've got forty-two couple here – that's eighty-four in all. When I first arrived at this hunt seven years ago we had a complete change of staff, which is most unusual. So there was no one within the kennels who knew any of the hounds. All I had was a piece of paper from the previous huntsman with ear numbers and names on it. You see, each hound has its number tattooed in its ears. So I had to stand there and call out the names and, as each one came forward, I had to try and print in my mind the way it looked and to attach it to that name. It took me three weeks to get hold of fifty couple in that way and now, of course, I know them all well and it's not a problem for me or the team.'

The huntsman has eyes that look you in the face, and a strong jaw. With a determination that would make his opponents think twice, he says: 'Everybody is entitled to their opinion about hunting. Obviously, mine is for the sport because it's my life. But I will talk to anybody about the do's and don'ts, the rights and wrongs of hunting, because I don't believe in violence of any sort. That proves nothing at all.'

Back at the kennels big, burly Bob, changed now into a brown overall, has a cuddle with a heavy old hound called Farnham. When he stands up on his hind legs, his front paws on his master's shoulders, the dog is as tall as the huntsman.

'Poor old Farnham was injured when he was a youngster and we stitched him up and made him well again,' explains Bob. 'He's never forgotten it. He comes up to me every day to say thank you and to give me a big wet kiss.'

While Bob circulates in the yard with a 'Goodboy' here and a 'Good fella' there, one of his colleagues is busy clothes-brushing and polishing the buttons of a row of pink coats hanging on

Bob Collins, huntsman, with some of his hounds

a rail outside in the autumn sunshine. The horses and hounds look on complacently, their day's work and exercise completed.

In August 1823 William Cobbett rode through Alresford, Bishops Sutton and Ropley Dean and reported in *Rural Rides*:

All along by the Itchen River, up to its very source at Ropley Dean, there are meadows; and this vale of meadows, which is about twenty-five miles in length and is, in some places, a mile wide is, at the point of which I am now speaking, only about twice as wide as my horse is long. This vale of Itchen is worthy of particular attention. There are few spots in England more fertile or more pleasant – and none, I believe, more healthy. The average width of the meadow is, I should think, a hundred rods at the least; and, if I am right in this conjecture, the vale contains about five thousand acres of meadows, a large part of which is regularly watered. The cornlands are excellent, and the farmhouses, to which those lands belong, are for the greater part under covert of the hills on the edge of the valley.

Terry Heathcote

The River Avon at Breamore

New Forest ponies grazing in autumn woodland

The West New Forest

The western side of Hampshire's New Forest runs from Woodgreen and Fordingbridge in the north down to the outskirts of Christchurch in the south. All the way, the wild heathland is flanked and watered by the River Avon as it loops its way through the pastures and meadowland past Ringwood to the sea. This westward edge of the Forest is not as well known as the Solent shore or the old centre round Lyndhurst and Brockenhurst. But that is no bad thing, because the tourists are fewer, the villages more hidden and remote and the forest animals less pestered and pampered. This is magnificent walking and riding country and the views across Hampshire and into Wiltshire and Dorset are as spacious and unspoilt as you could hope for in this overcrowded island.

Because this special place has been in existence for nearly a thousand years, its inhabitants have a sense of continuity and tradition which people from cities may find hard to comprehend. But the fact that land and family history have been passed down from generation to generation gives these ancient areas a stability, a purpose and a meaning denied to less favoured parts of the country. And it is something for which no amount of education or material advantage can be a substitute.

Early on a September morning, Jonathan Gerelli, the agister for the West New Forest, and his team are busy getting ready for one of their autumn pony drifts. At this time of the year all the commoners' horses and their new foals, born in the spring, are rounded up and looked over. The sick or injured ones are treated, and the young ones branded and tail-marked and then released back on to the Forest until next time. Such events have been taking place for centuries and are as typical of the New Forest as its wild heathland and its ancient woodlands: 'First thing this morning early we have to set up what we call the

Jonathan Gerelli, New Forest agister

pound. It's a stout stockade made up of a number of heavy, wooden sections, and it has to be put up in the different areas where we are going to catch the ponies. We do this so that we can hold the animals in a confined space, get hold of them more

59

easily, cut their tails to show that they've been seen to and carry out all the other things that need doing to them after twelve months out in the wild.'

The men have built these crushes before. For them, it is like redoing a favourite jigsaw puzzle. They sweat and curse gently as they manoeuvre the heavy timbers into position. Jonathan is tall and slim, brown-haired and with a cheeky grin. His face is finely chiselled and he speaks with a soft, Hampshire accent. Watched by a scattering of New Forest commoners and other curious spectators, the horsemen are mounting up in an isolated glade where horse-boxes outnumber people and dogs outnumber both. Jonathan leads an athletic, white stallion down the ramp of his box: 'Mine is a grey Arab, fourteen years old now and a strong and agile horse. He's good for this job and he's clever too, because he's learnt from previous round-ups. He sometimes thinks he knows better than I do and perhaps he does too. He sometimes wants to take me his way rather than my way, but we normally work it out' – and he chuckles 'We've got a good thing going between us and it usually comes together all right in the end.'

The horse stands proudly in the forest clearing – the early sun reflecting off its white flanks. Its head and tail are held high with pride – the tail erect after centuries of training and breeding in the desert to protect the rider from pursuing arrows. A quiet stream winds its way seawards at the side of the surrounding trees. The first autumn leaves float daintily downstream. After a brief consultation about where to ride and find the big bunches of wild ponies that have to be rounded up in this sector of the Forest, the riders move off together – hard-bitten men with wise, lined faces, experienced in the ways of the Forest and in the dangers of galloping across the rough heathland: 'We have about forty of these drifts or round-ups in the course of the year. That covers the whole New Forest and allows us to have a look as close as possible at all the ponies on it. We start about the middle of August and go on up to the beginning of November. The idea is to catch and to have a look at all the ponies on the Forest. Obviously you have problems and some get away. But only a few because we have drifts in every part of the Forest. It's a kind of once-a-year health check. They have their tails cut and that's to show that they've been seen to and have been paid for to run on the common land. A lot of the ponies are wormed, foals are branded to show who their owners are, and then they are all released back into the wild.'

Among the oaks, beeches and conifers and across the heather and gorse echo the sounds and calls and shouts of the riders. There is the clattering of hooves on gravel, the high-pitched whinnying of foals separated briefly from their mothers, the snapping of wood underfoot and the gurgling and gushing of woodland streams. A disturbed pheasant screeches overhead. A jay clatters its alarm. Horses and riders emerge from the thickets. Wild ponies appear and then double back in fright. Soon, on a broad Forest lawn a bunch of thirty or forty tough-looking horses canter steadily away, followed by a tight semi-circle of riders. There is no escape and it is a sight as old as history: 'Certainly, even before there were these organised round-ups, New Forest commoners used to get together and go out in groups and catch the horses they wanted to have a look at. And that's where the pony drifts started from. It's slowly built on from there to what it is today. I love every minute of it. These are good days. It's exciting. You're riding through this wooded country and heathland – very often at high speed. It can be hazardous but that adds to the thrill of it. And it's an important job as well – to round up the animals and to have the chance to look them over closely.'

It is a stampede. The horses are herded pell-mell into a rough funnel of bushes and bystanders. It leads to the pound, which the men had built earlier. Red-hot branding irons stick dangerously out of an open fire. There is shouting, kicking, whistling, swearing, the cracking of whips and much rushing back and forth by men and animals: 'I suppose, to an outsider, it must look like chaos. On the whole though we know what we are doing, so it usually goes all right in the end. And the main thing is that the work gets done and that the ponies get seen to.'

It is no picnic inside the pound with half-a-dozen wild ponies corralled in there at any one time. Hard, fearless men climb in and brand the youngsters, which react and shudder a good second after the iron has been applied. The smell of burning hair and flesh floats through the air. Worming tubes are thrust down unwilling throats. Tails are severely cut while hooves lash out and flail. The commoners risk being kicked or crushed at every moment. But they don't seem to care: 'The ponies are very wild. They live a natural life out in the Forest all year round and in all weathers. Although each one is owned by someone, they are left out in the open to their own devices. So they are untamed and unbroken animals and in no way domesticated. We have a number of permanent pens built in some places but not everywhere, and that's why we have to construct these mobile ones. They have to be well built because these horses are strong and excited. You just have to get hold of them as best you can when they have to be branded or wormed, and you get knocked about quite a bit and you get kicked and trodden on. But that's one of the hazards of the job' – and he laughs as he plunges back into the melee: 'I've always been in the Forest. I was born and bred here. And I can't see myself being settled anywhere else. I love the Forest life. My family are all here – and, of course, the animals. I just love it. It's really great.'

The released ponies trot placidly off one by one through tangles of bramble bushes and out into the early autumn landscape. Behind them the bedlam continues.

New Forest keeper Derek Thomson, has worked for the Forestry Commission for thirty-one years. He has a whole assortment of jobs and duties, many of them undefined and instinctive. One of his more unusual responsibilities is for the snake and lizard pits near Lyndhurst: 'I know they don't appeal to everyone, but I like snakes because I've been living and working with them and admiring them for the last three decades.'

Derek is a stocky, independent man with a round face and greying hair. He is accompanied everywhere by a strong red dog. When he is out walking the woodland rides round his cottage at Holiday Hill he usually has a much-used twelve-bore shotgun tucked under his arm. But now he lifts up the edge of one of the covers over the snake pits and climbs carefully down, so as not to harm or disturb his precious charges. There are plenty of them here for him to examine and to make sure that they are all in good fettle. The adders have dramatic jagged, black and yellow patterns down their backs and sides. Their tongues flicker but there is no menace: 'I can't really remember very clearly whether, when I first came to the forest thirty-one or thirty-two years ago, I had this interest in reptiles then or not. But certainly, since being here and helping to build this reptilliary where they are kept, my passion for the creatures has increased year by year. You have to treat them with respect, of course, but, providing that you do, they are not dangerous. I know that out here in the woods the old timers often say how aggressive and dangerous adders are. But that isn't really the case. The snakes are shy and retiring and would much prefer to keep out of your way. They are not waiting in trees to spring out on you and get you by the throat as some folk would have you believe.'

Derek Thomson, Forest keeper, talking about deer

Terry Heathcote

61

The keeper bends and gently picks up a tiny, patterned snake from under an overhanging rock. He lays it on the palm of his hand. It is the same length as his longest finger. Its arrowhead markings are clear and strong: 'This is a baby adder, born about a week or ten days ago. It's doing fine. Soon it will be going into hibernation. They're usually born in early September. Then, in the autumn, as the weather begins to get colder, they slip away into their special places to spend the winter asleep, lucky things.'

Another of Derek's regular jobs is to keep an eye on and feed the deer at Bolderwood. Up there, at the top of the Ornamental Drive, he hauls paper bags full of corn and meal from the back of his forester's van. Thirty or forty magnificent antlered deer watch and wait timidly. They have tan and white speckled coats and those distinctive white rumps, which bob hypnotically up and down as they run away from you. As Derek pours out the feed in long lines on to the Forest lawn he calls out to the deer, 'Come on – come on, then.' They approach tentatively – one step at a time – the animals at the back taking courage from the ones in front: 'These are all fallow deer – the most common of our deer in the New Forest. This time of the year, the rut is approaching so they are quite nervous. They are shying and jumping about. Some of them are getting aggressive. If you look closely at the older fallow bucks you'll see that their necks are quite swollen. This is an indication that their mating time is close at hand. And towards the end of this month, September, the deer will leave the Forest lawns and go out into their favourite rutting areas. There they set up their rutting stands, where the stags will start to mate with the does for next year's fawns.'

He stands and watches from beside his vehicle as the animals move forward to feed. When the brave ones arrive, the more fearful ones take courage and follow. Soon they are all feeding contentedly. But they still glance up swiftly every now and again on the look-out for danger. Antlers and heads and hooves make a moving mosaic against the green of the grass: 'I'm a country man through and through. I've always loved living and working in these open spaces – particularly with the animals and, above all, the snakes and these deer. I

come across birds and all sorts of other creatures too on my daily rounds. I wouldn't be tempted to move from the New Forest under any circumstances.'

As he speaks, a large, dark coloured buck lashes out at his neighbour. He lowers his head, the antlers pointing menacingly. Derek watches quietly, affection mixed with sadness in his face.

A crowd gathers to watch the feeding of deer at Bolderwood

Brian and Angie Wilson, from Linford, are two of the commoners whose animals will soon be rounded up for their annual check-up by the agister Jonathan Gerrelli and his team. Both can trace their families back for five hundred years in the area and, as well as ponies, they keep cattle, pigs and pigeons. Smallholdings like this have been here since medieval times, and people like the Wilsons have kept alive the old Forest customs and fashions which contribute so much to its character today. On a damp September afternoon Angie is on horseback, where she spends much of her day, rounding up and bringing in a bunch of twenty or thirty cattle. She has to drive them across a fast-running stream, which their leaders are hesitant to tackle. Strong of body and firm of face, Angie, astride a fine bay horse, keeps the beasts on the move, wheeling back and forth like a cowboy: 'The main reason we do it is that this is the life which we were brought up for. I was born and bred here and it just means everything to me. It may sound ridiculous to outsiders but, if I go away half a day, all I do is yearn to come back. People say that I'm lucky to be able to ride out across the Forest like this – and they're right. But the truth is that it's second nature to me. I get on a horse's back to fetch the cattle in and I don't even realise that I'm doing it. It's just like walking would be to someone else – an everyday, every-hour occurrence. Of course, it's an especially lovely life in the summer time. But you should try it in the wind and the frost and the cold and the rain in the winter months. That sorts things and people out a bit. I still wouldn't want to do anything else. But this wouldn't suit everyone, I assure you. It can be very hard work indeed.' The fine, fat cattle move steadily across the meadow towards their home fields. They realise where the boss is taking them now and they know the way.

Back at her home, Angie is bucket-feeding some sturdy white cross landrace pigs in sties beside the barn. She is a tall, blonde woman with short-cut hair and a determined and amused face: 'Much to Brian's disgust, my pigs have become pet pigs. In spite of that and to keep the balance, we put one in the freezer from time to time. So he can't complain too much. This year the sow farrowed and she only had two. So that was a disappointment. Mind you, she had one male and one female piglet, so the population can still go on increasing. But, when I get a litter that size, it doesn't go down very well. In addition, it means that we're not making much money from them, I'm afraid.'

Brian is a strong man with a dark face and brooding eyes. You would not choose to pick a quarrel with him. Like Angie, he has a warm Hampshire twang in his voice. At the top of one of his meadows, he is wielding a sledge-hammer as if it was a toy, and carrying out some much-needed fencing repairs: 'What we have is a living – not much more than that. But it's also a way of life – and it's out of doors. And that's the place to be. Fresh air never killed anybody. You've got freedom. You've got the birds and the animals. You have the wind, the water, the sun, the rain, the frost – everything. It's far better than working indoors, I promise you.'

Angie joins him to lend a hand. As they move steadily up the fence post by post she manages the wire strainers and, with a smile, asks her husband why she always finds herself doing the heavy jobs and carrying the big tools. She speaks of her man with affection, pulling his leg as she must often do: 'Quite honestly, I believe that being a commoner's wife is one of the hardest jobs there is. First of all you've got to help with the animals, no matter how you feel, how tired you may be and whatever the weather. It can be five o'clock in the morning to twelve o'clock at night. Next on the list comes his stomach – or his belly as we call it here in the Forest. No commoner is happy unless he is fed first. And it's always got to be good, old-fashioned meat and three veg. Then comes yourself – and, to be honest, you don't think of yourself any more by then because you're too tired. And you just go on up to bed and that's the end of your day.' But she laughs as she speaks, and you can tell that she loves it and her man, and that they get on fine together. Around them the Forest prepares itself for the night.

Apple pulp is exotic fare for New Forest animals. But there is a particular reason why Barry and Sue Topp, fourth-generation commoners from Pound Lane in Burley, have plenty of it to feed to their cows. For they are professional cider-makers in an area which was once famous for its potent apple juice. Nowadays, the Topp's farmhouse cider is sold far and wide across the South of England. Barry is a dark man with a mop of black hair and wearing a lumberjack's check shirt. Watched by an inquisitive crowd of white ducks, he is loading box after box of green apples into a wooden hopper, which is precariously fixed above a vintage belt-driven pulper. The Fordson Major tractor, which drives the machinery, is the

Barry Topp, cider maker

divided into two types – bitter sweets and bitter sharps. The main area for those apples is about an hour away from here across the border into Somerset. I work three large orchards in Somerset, and so a good seventy to eighty per cent of the apples we are pressing here are specially grown there for us as a proper cider fruit. So it's no use, really, using any old apples off any old trees.'

Pulp continues to pour into pans beneath the crusher. Some juice is already in evidence and wasps roam greedily around. The long belt from the tractor lurches and slaps. Nearby in a barn is the press itself – a huge, menacing creation. Giant nuts and bolts crown layer upon layer of wooden slats, straw and sacking. The pulp is carried in and spread out between each layer: 'We're pressing using the old-fashioned method here. It goes through straw as it used to in Thomas Hardy's time. As each "cheese", as we call it (or layers of pulped apples), is finished pressing and there is no more juice in it, it's either fed to the cattle, which are very happy with it, or turned into compost and used as fertiliser on the land. So there's no waste. We use fresh straw to strain it through from an organic farm up on Salisbury Plain. I know that it's not been sprayed, so there's no danger of chemicals or other additives affecting the juice. And, after it's pressed, the liquid is run straight into former whiskey barrels with an element of whiskey still in them. So it increases its alcoholic strength because of the residues of whiskey in the barrels. I buy them direct from a distillery in Scotland.'

The activity is intense. Blue crates of pulped and crushed applies are carried back and forth. Bundles of straw and sacking bulge under the pressure. It is a warm September afternoon and, as the juice flows serenely from the press through the sacks and the straw, into the containers beneath, it carries the cool sound of a woodland stream: 'Tomorrow morning we'll lift the main beam of the press and trim down the edges of the material – the bits that have been squeezed out by the pressure. Then we'll build up another three or four layers of straw and sacking on the top with pulp in between and screw it down again.' The big man sweats and strains as he levers backwards and forwards on a mighty cog-wheel, putting

same age, at least, as the crusher. Wheels spin, belts slap, broken apples fall wantonly into a collecting tub: 'Traditional New Forest apples were mainly acidic and produced a sharp cider – a very powerful one too. But it's too sour for today's tastes. A decent drink needs proper cider fruit, which are increasing pressure on the fruit pulp beneath: 'There'll be roughly one and a half tons of pulp in the press and, squeezed down, we'll get about five barrels or hogsheads of juice out of the cheese.'

In the cool and quiet of the barn next door, Sue Topp is pouring cider into a rustic container from one of a row of five-foot-tall wooden barrels for a waiting customer. By itself the smell is intoxicating: 'The apples we are pressing today are an early variety called Northern Sweet. It makes what we call a true, harvest scrumpy. It will ferment very quickly because it's still quite mild at this time of the year. And it should be ready for drinking in six weeks' time.'

Out in the field beyond the buildings the cattle are lining up, patiently waiting for their next pulp ration.

Tiptoe is close to New Milton at the south-western corner of the New Forest. Here Nick Rayner farms the thin soil and tries to make a living from his beef cattle. But his pride and joy is his team of Shire horses, which he uses instead of a tractor whenever the job allows it. Nick sometimes says that he would rather sell his tractor than one of his heavy horses and that, until you've worked with one, you cannot know how good and how willing they are. He is a tall man with greying hair and a perky hat on his head. He has an upright carriage and there is warmth in his face and in his voice: 'I don't think I was ever fit for anything other than farming – wouldn't have wanted to have been either. But it's what I've got used to and I wouldn't change it for anything. It's our way of life down here. We don't make a vast profit, but it's what we want to do. So we've got our little bit of independence.'

Nick is carrying a bale of hay on the end of a pitchfork slung over his shoulder, to some cattle in an open yard. The cows move forward and munch appreciatively. They look sleek and contented. They watch as their master leads a handsome Shire horse with a white nose and forehead into the farmyard. It is pulling behind it a smart blue cart with red shafts. It is loaded with more hay and has Nick's name and address carefully stencilled on its front: 'We've always had heavy horses on the farm.

I suppose that we've had them here for thirty years and more – and I kept 'em before that. Then my grandfather had some before me, so it goes way back. You grow up with them, you see. It's something that's within you. And, yes, I would rather have them than a machine. But we've got tractors too because you must have them nowadays, though I'd rather work with a horse any day of the week.'

The animal's great feathered feet are planted firmly on the earth. It has huge, muscled shoulders and thighs – an equine Goliath. Nick is taking the load of hay out through the wooden farmyard gates and on to the open forest to feed to a motley array of his animals – ponies and cattle, which are in the wild for some of the time during the summer and autumn months: 'The first time I was ever allowed to drive out like this on my own with a heavy horse, I thought I was king of the heap. Proud as Punch I was. It was the only thing I had ever wanted to do. But, looking back, that was rather silly and I suppose I was fairly insignificant in those days. Gradually, over time, you progress naturally from one horse to two – then three and then four. And, in the end, you hope to have got it all together and you can do what you like with them.'

The Shire strides out across the Forest lawn under his own steam and with no hands on reins or halter while Nick stands unsteadily on the back of the cart forking out hay in a long trail across the grass. Ponies of all colours and a few cattle scramble for the food as it falls to the ground. At last some kind of pecking order is established and they take their places along the line and feed peaceably: 'We usually bring all the ponies in at night. They know the routine and they're queueing up to get in at sundown. We feed them hay and then, in the daytime, we let them out on the Forest and give them a bit more hay because it's September now and the grass has mostly stopped growing. Then they come back at night and wait for us to let 'em in. We get our neighbours' ponies coming along to help themselves to our hay out here as well. But then that's something we commoners have always had to put up with. We always will have to. You can't sort 'em out. If you get a few other people's animals taking your grub, well, so what? Let's hope they've got some of ours feeding off their hay.' A grey colt, halfway down the line, sucks milk from its tan-coloured mother as she munches on the sweet-smelling dried grass – a great beard and mustache of hay slowly disappears into her mouth. Her eyes are half-closed in apparent ecstasy.

It is late morning and up the farm lane Nick is driving two black cart horses with matching, white socks. They are pulling behind them an ancient muck-spreader loaded with manure from the cattle yard. The metal wheels clang and clatter on the hard surface of the road. Pebbles pop and fly from beneath hooves and wheels. Nick turns left into a green meadow and starts spreading the dung. It is not a good implement to walk too close behind: 'This piece of machinery is made by Massey

Terry Heathcote

Nick Rayner, with one of his heavy horses

Harris. It came over to England with the American Lease-Lend scheme during the war. It's as old as can be and nearly on its last legs. We just keep on mending it and bodging it, hoping it will go on for a year or two yet. And we're trying to get another one from America because, believe it or not, they still make them now out there. It's surprising what you can get through in a day with two of these Shire horses. When it comes to ploughing you can do an acre a day with them – and that's heavy work. By the end of that session you will have walked eleven miles up and down behind them. With jobs like harrowing or drilling corn, they can manage ten to fifteen acres a day – but you're sitting up on the machine then, so you don't get your exercise. You just get bumped about a bit. It depends on the size and length of your fields and the distance of each run how much you get through in a day.' As Nick sits high behind the rounded black rumps of the majestic animals, the wheel at the back of the spreader flings the lumps of dung high in a cascade behind him: 'I don't think I'd want to live anywhere else after all these years here. I've travelled across England and I've never really found anywhere quite like this. So I think I'll have to stay here.' As the vehicle trundles away up the meadow a buzzard mews as it soars overhead, the sun touching the colours on its pinions.

As smallholders and commoners Lena Martin's family has inhabited this part of the Forest for generations. Circumstances have obliged Lena to live in Ringwood, where she bought her small house sight unseen. But she still owns a meadow close to where her family once lived. So every day except Sunday and in all weathers, Lena makes the ten-mile round trip by bike to Rye Close – even though she was born during the first decade of the century. Here she keeps things trim and tidy, looks after her New Forest pony, Penny, and her foal and watches and enjoys the birds and the wildlife on and around her precious patch of land. Lena is a little old lady, but tough as teak. She wears a jaunty tweed hat and jacket. She has a sharp face, with bright eyes and spectacles. Beneath there is a strong and determined mouth and jaw. She sharpens her hedging hook with a well-worn whetstone and starts methodically cutting and clearing long grass and under-growth beside a hedge: 'I'm a loner. I like to be on my own because I can stand out here under a tree if I see some deer out feeding in the open. I stop quite still and pull my hat down over my forehead and almost over my eyes. I always wear gloves, to cover the white of my hands, and dark-coloured clothes. I stand like a post and they come quite near and I can watch them and enjoy them at my leisure.'

Lena brings out and shows a slim hazel walking-stick with a catapult V at the top. This is her constant companion on her walks: 'I always use my thumb-stick when I'm out in the Forest. I never go for a stroll without it. It's not so much for protection from snakes or dogs. Most of them are shy anyway. But, if I'm crossing one of the many bogs out this way, I can use it to feel the ground ahead of me to find out whether the surface is firm enough for me to step over it. It's important to remember that there are some dangerous bogs in this part of the world. Just as valuable as the stick if you're crossing marshy ground is to look carefully around until you find a narrow track where the ponies and deer have been. If you follow that, you can be pretty sure that you will be safe. But you need the stick as well because of holes or other obstacles.'

Later Lena sits by a spitting campfire on which a blackened tin kettle is bubbling away. She makes herself tea and sips it appreciatively. A robin watches from a bush, cocking its head to one side: 'The wildlife is wonderful out here. That's why I come really. While I sit boiling my kettle, I often get woodpeckers down the bottom of my field. I've had a fox come along to take a look at me from time to time. And, of course, the deer come in here every night. They help themselves to my grass and whatever else they can find. I'm pleased even if it is what my ponies should be having. And oh no, I couldn't live all my life in town – not possibly. I've always been in the country. It's been my whole life, you see – all that time – not far from here – always.' And the old eyes are moist as she looks off into the distance across the heathland to the woods beyond.

In September the glory of autumn in the New Forest is still a few weeks away. But people and animals alike begin to feel its coming as the evenings draw in. There's a chill in the air and the skies are lower and less open as the heat of summer begins to fade. The best of the grazing on the thin, sandy soil is now gone and ponies and cattle prepare themselves for their meagre winter rations. Soon cottage chimneys will be smoking again and the Forest people will settle down into their cold, wet-weather routines. For a thousand years the patterns and the landscapes have remained much the same – untroubled by time and fortune and human invention. For a thousand years more may the splendour of the New Forest be allowed to continue its wild, windswept and unmanicured existence in the midst of one of the most civilised stretches of man-made countryside on earth.

Back of the Wight

To purists, 'Back of the Wight' is a designated sixteen-mile long stretch of the island's south-west coast, reaching from St Catherine's Point up towards the Needles. To those less inclined to strict guidelines, it is used to describe almost anywhere along the southern coast – for who can resist such an evocative title? Even during a gale-swept and stormy January week it feels here as though you have travelled to warmer climes overseas – as indeed you have – to reach this haven of calm and quiet civilisation. And islanders know that there is no comparison between their patch and the rest of the United Kingdom. It is a secret, which they are happy to keep to themselves as much as they can.

Foreigners from the mainland and from further afield too have also noticed the difference. In placid mood, Karl Marx wrote that 'you can stroll here for hours, enjoying both sea and mountain air at the same time.' And Charles Dickens was of the opinion that 'from the top of the highest down, there are views, which are only to be equalled on the Genoese shore of the Mediterranean.' Long time resident, J.B. Priestley thought that 'any man from America or Australia might take one glance at the island as something on a map, and then decide to give it a couple of hours. But you can spend days and days exploring the Isle of Wight, which, if you are really interested, begins magically enlarging itself for you.' None of this, of course, would come as news to the islanders who know that all of it and much more is true of their unique home.

The beach at Ventnor has been run by the Blake family since the 1830s. At that time it was just a handful of cottages along the shoreline. But the Victorian fashion for bathing brought boom times to the town, and its fair weather still brings summer visitors in their thousands. In January the crowds have

Ventnor in January

Terry Heathcote

69

vanished, but there are still crabs, lobsters and other fish for Geoff Blake and his team to catch and to sell – providing that the conditions allow them to go to sea. Geoff is a sturdy, broad-shouldered, handsome young man with a mop of curly, black hair and with an open, friendly face and straight eyes, which have the possibility of hardness in them if circumstances demand it. He is clad in a heavy, woollen sweater against the wind, which is whipping the white horses off the top of the waves. A couple of miles further up the coast foam is being carried up over the top of two hundred foot cliffs by the force of the blast. Out at sea a naval frigate is making heavy weather of the swell – its bow sinking below the waves until it seems that it must be going to plunge beneath the surface. Then, miraculously, it holds and judders upwards again in a nail-biting resurrection: 'Unfortunately it was blowing a force ten gale yesterday, and it was so bad that we had to take out boat round to Bembridge for protection. We'd be mad to go out from here at Ventnor today. It's far too rough. But we managed to go to sea first thing this morning early from the relative calm at Bembridge and we brought in some crab and cod. So, at least we've got some fish in to keep us going until this fierce wind dies down a bit.'

Just along the harbour road Geoff and his family have their boat and fishing workshops and their cooking and preparation rooms. He lifts the lid from a cauldron of boiling water. The smell is of the sea and of the freshest of fresh crabs. Inside there are scores of the creatures, all well cooked and their shells the colour of rusty metal. Some of them are a foot across. The fisherman extracts them one at a time with some wooden tongs and places them in a waiting crate: 'During the summer season we got very busy indeed. The pubs are screaming at us for crabmeat during the hot, sunny weather through July and August. We just have to put a lot of hours in to catch enough of everything to keep the market going.'

Inside, on a clean, kitchen worktop a slim and attractive girl with blonde ringlets and swiftly-moving hands is extracting the crabmeat from the claws and the shells and is putting it into large bowls, ready for the customers. Every now and again she cracks and shatters the back shells with a hammer.

This is fresh crabmeat as it is meant to be: 'We can't compete with supermarkets on price, but we can on quality. We are daily fresh – quite often landed at 9 or 10 o'clock in the morning. We have the crab that's caught that day cooked by midday ready to be sold in our shop here or to be delivered to the pubs, where it goes straight into sandwiches or salads for their lunchtime customers.'

While the girl works on, reducing crate after crate of crabs to what is edible and filling dustbins with the rejected shell, Geoff is next door in his boat and workshop. It is a marvellous muddle of dinghies, ropes, tools, bits of engines, oars and paddles, lobster pots, flags, buoys, boilers, buckets and stepladders: 'When we can't go out fishing because of the weather, there's always plenty to do in here.' He's busy using his strength fitting hefty rubber tubing round a modern lobster pot to protect it from the surging water and sea currents bashing it against undersea rocks or on the bottom: 'We have all our precious pots to repair and maintain. We use traditional, English Channel, inkwell pots – the sort you will see in fishing ports all along the south coast. They last probably five or

Geoff Blake, fisherman

six years if you look after them and try to ensure that they are not set up in the more exposed places when these gales come in. If you make a mistake about that, then they can be cast adrift or smashed to pieces. We have about 250 of them, which we haul daily. So there's always plenty to do keeping them in good repair.'

Down on Ventnor beach, on the edge of the giant surf, Geoff's father, a wise fisherman of the old school, is walking his rough-haired dog and throwing stones for it to chase: 'My Dad started fishing here in the 1940s and '50s after he came out of his National Service. Before that, the beach – deckchairs, rowing boats, looking after the visitors – had been his main business. But, as that tailed off with so many people going overseas, he did more of the fishing. And, as I began to grow up and became big enough, I started going out with him from the time I was nine or ten years old. Then, when I got to be about twenty, I took on the fishing and Dad was happy to go back to running the beach.'

Without any reservation at all, it is possible to recommend the taste and the texture of the crabmeat, which you can buy from the Blakes' wooden shop in the centre of the Ventnor seafront. It makes what is available in supermarkets taste like wet sawdust. It is, quite simply, delicious: 'Our little hut on the promenade, where we sell whole crabs or tubs of crab-meat, gets very busy during the season. A lot of locals come there regularly and then the visitors on top of that. Add to that our pub trade and we've got plenty to keep us busy. Sometimes, on a good day, we're running backwards and for-wards like yo-yos. We definitely have a future for what we do here, if we market what we produce ourselves. That way we're in control of our business. There's a lot of downward pressure on crab prices, particularly on the bulk markets. But we can make a living quite happily if we can retail.'

The sound and weight of the heavy waves roaring ashore shakes the foundations of the shop. The gulls floating over-head wheel north and head inland to quieter climes.

It is not just the much publicised dinosaurs and the scenery which have made the south-west coast of the Isle of Wight famous. It also shelters a treasure trove of fossils, dating back tens of millions of years. It was this that tempted fossil hunter, Martin Simpson, from Cheshire to come here nearly twenty years ago – and today he spends his time searching for, uncovering and polishing these fascinating pieces of the island's history. The tall, tough man strides cautiously along a beach, where the rollers nearly topple him from time to time. Every now and again he has to put out a hand to steady himself against the cliff: 'When we get storms like this on the back of the island, that's the best time to collect fossils, because the weight of the water does a lot of the work for you. This morning I've been down in the wild weather looking for ammonites – big ones if possible. They're great, round shells like the wheels of a Mini. And the sea has washed away the clay from the foot of the cliffs and, if you are lucky and come across one, you can see it sticking out of the mud like a car tyre. That's what I'm always on the look-out for – that magic moment when you see one poking out from the clay.'

He stops, steadies himself against the raging surf and grabs hold of a hefty ammonite. Scrabbling with his hands he digs the brown clay out from around it. Lashed by wind and waves, he holds it up in triumph. He is a strong, bearded man with wild hair, enthusiastic eyes and traces of the Midlands still in his voice. He is wearing heavy, yellow fisherman's oil-skins. His find is so heavy that he has to perch it on his knee to take the weight as he talks: 'This is it. It may not be the best weather for sunbathing. But it's brilliant for me and my job, because the sea has come up in the night and done all the work. It's scrubbed the cliff clean of clay and this ammonite has been washed out. It's a fantastic one – nearly two feet across and about ten inches deep. The way things are going at the moment, we're losing about three feet of cliff a year here. That's not so good for the Isle of Wight. But it's great for fos-sil-hunters. There are hundreds – probably thousands – of fossils like this one buried deep under the cliffs. But it's rare that you get them so clean or so simply. That's one more for me.' And he sets out for home carrying his heavy burden in triumph. Behind him the surf surges unrelentingly: 'Everything on the island is about a hundred million years old under the chalk. The whole of the back of the island is made up of this clay and sand. And, because it's so soft and yielding, the fossils emerge in these great, hard boulders and sometimes just lie on the beach waiting to be picked up.'

Back at his fossil shop, Martin has cleaned himself up and sits at a workbench in the warmth. He works deftly on an ammonite with a metal mallet and chisel. Earlier he had cleaned off the clay under a hose: 'When I get the fossils back to the workshop, the first thing I have to do is clean them. Everything on the beach has, of course, got salt on it and, if you don't get that out, it will crumble. So you soak it for two days and then you can start to chisel it. When you get right down to the middle, you can use engravers to get the middle out. Then they're ready to be sold.'

The place is a treasure-trove of multi-coloured stones and rocks, jewels and fossils, skeletons and shells. Martin walks over and sits beside an enormous ammonite – the size of a front wheel of a tractor: 'They come in all shapes and sizes, these chaps. They're shells and they're shaped in a spiral. This one here is the biggest I've ever found. It's a bit like the one I pulled out of the mud this-morning, but about twice the size. And, if you're lucky, sometimes they are made of crystal and, when they are, you can slice them in half and polish them. Commercially, those are the ones I can sell best. They do good business for me. They're most attractive and, on them, you can clearly see all the chambers getting smaller and smaller as they go down to the middle of the shell.'

Martin moves across to one of the crowded shelves at the back of his shop and collects two chunks of orange and brown, shiny, plastic-like stone from the top shelf. They are dusty, but plastic they certainly are not: 'These are two pieces of amber. One is still as rough as when it was found and the other has been polished. Amber is fossilised tree sap – about a hundred million years old. And the interesting thing is that the fossils inside them – the flies and spiders and the other bugs, which are caught in the sap when it was sticky and coming out of the tree – are still perfect and well-preserved after that amazing length of time. And you can see them all clearly, as well as the small pieces of leaf and other insects. Finds like this are popular as jewellery, but they're scientifically important as well.'

From another shelf he reaches for a black, pointed spike – smooth and shiny – as long as his index finger and as fat as his thumb at the base: 'As well as fossilised shells and all the other things which we discover along this coast, we also find dinosaurs. They're mostly in bits and pieces, but this is a whole and single tooth. It was a meat-eating creature, because it has serrated edge down the end for sawing away at the flesh.' He takes the tooth over to a piece of rock, which must weigh a hundredweight or two and which has wedged into it what looks like a piece of the blade of a unique band saw: 'This is just a single tooth but what I've got here is part of the jaw of something, which was about fifty feet long and lived in the sea. It had these enormous brown and white teeth with sharp, black tips and it's called a plesiosaurus. It had a long neck, a short tail and four large paddles to swim with. And that's what people think the Loch Ness Monster is. So, if they find one, it will have teeth like these.' The gale shakes the frame and the windows of the building. Out at sea, the only monsters in sight are the waves.

Martin Simpson, fossil hunter, at work on an ammonite

Terry Heathcote

Son of the poet, Alfred Noyes, Hugh Noyes has lived on the undercliff to the west of Ventnor since he was one year old. Once he was a journalist in London.

But today, he and his family run a flourishing and exotic rare breeds farm with a collection of birds, animals and creatures the like of which the Isle of Wight has certainly never seen before. Hugh is a tall, grey-haired man, slim and stooping. There is a touch of Alastair Sim about him. He wears jeans, a warm coat and black gumboots as he feeds a bunch of tawny goats. Looking on enviously are some Aukole cattle from Africa with horns like motorbike handlebars: 'Our land is on what is called the undercliff of the Isle of Wight – a part of the land, which fell away from the rest of it several million years ago. As a result of the high cliffs, which now stand behind our meadows, we have an unusually mild climate, which means that we can grow exotic plants and keep rare animals out of doors, which would be impossible to do in less favourable parts of the country. This new enterprise started about ten years ago when quotas on milk production came into being and we found that the quota, which had been allotted to us, was completely uneconomical. So we decided that all we could do was to go into a different line of country and open a rare breeds park for the holiday-makers on the Isle of Wight.'

Hugh stands with a bucket in his hand in a waterlogged meadow. He is surrounded by deer, long-horned and shaggy sheep and a whole array of other animals. He is giving special attention to a superb, tawny stag – or perhaps it is the stag which is giving the attention to its master: 'He's called Boswell. He's a red deer stag. These red deer seem to become very tame indeed in these controlled circumstances. Boswell sometimes gets a little too tame for some of our visitors. He's so friendly that he walks up and nudges them. And, if you have ten sharp points on the sides and ends of your antlers, that's not always entirely appreciated by some of the people who visit our park.'

The animals mill around him – an exotic mixture of castes and colours, each trying to get its fair share of the bucket. In the heavy wind – aftermath of yesterday's gales – Hugh works high on a cliff-top meadow, feeding concentrate nuts to a whole array of cattle and some tiny ponies: 'Of the four-legged variety, I should think that we have got about thirty breeds of cattle, sheep, pigs, ponies, goats, llamas and horses.

Hugh Noyes, rare breeds farmer

Terry Heathcote

And, in addition to that, I would guess that we have a hundred species of poultry, waterfowl, peacocks, pheasants and those sorts of things.'

In a well barricaded enclosure with a pond and a stream,

73

sleek, inquisitive otters are being fed chunks of fish. They seize them and dash away with their prizes, crunching at the bones and the flesh with their strong jaws and pointed teeth: 'One person, who visited us, wrote back afterwards and described me as Doctor Dolittle of the Isle of Wight. It may not be particularly flattering, but it implies at least that we are at one with all the birds and animals, which we keep here. We certainly love them and we do our utmost to look after them in the best way that we can. Living in such a place, we always wonder when we go away on holiday, why we bother to travel. Because, to my mind, the Isle of Wight beats almost anywhere else in the world.' As an otter attacks its last chunk of fish with great relish, the sun goes down in a fury of red clouds.

Even using artistic licence, nobody could claim that Newchurch is 'Back of the Wight'. But that is where stonemasons Dave Hailstone and Dave Crouch with their fixer, Andy Jacobs from Chale on the south-west coast were working in early January. So that is where we went to find them, smartening up with their age-old skills the fine village church. Dave Crouch, a black baseball cap perched above a tightly tied pony tail and wire-rimmed spectacles and, in spite of the exercise of his labours, well clad against the cold, wields a round-headed mallet the size of a boxing-glove. He is concentrating on the stonework of the south facing windows – much assaulted by sea air and wind and weather: 'Being an islander and working on these old, island buildings, it's satisfying for us because you're keeping places like this church up and running and using natural materials to do it. They're the same types of stone in fact as the men used when they put them up in the first place. One of the important things in this job is to be accurate when you're cutting your templates. You've got to be sure that the pattern is right and that you're copying perfectly the original profile of the building and its stonework. And then you need to learn to take your time, because it's a slow process. And you have to be careful how you do it and what you do, because, if you make a mistake with a big bit of stone, you have to chuck it away and start again.'

Dave Hailstone wears protective goggles against the flying chips of stone and is warmly wrapped like his colleagues. He is a broad-shouldered man and his work with his mallet is meticulous – never hitting the chisel too strongly: 'We have six or seven windows to repair in this church and they are all major jobs. The one we're working on at the moment is the full bit with mullions and a head and odds and sods round the outside. The trouble with the work is that the stone is quite badly damaged and it's not surprising because these windows date back to 1726. Another one which we'll come to later, is a lot older than that and we shall probably have to replace the whole window there. The other factor is that these are big windows – ten or twelve feet tall. And so, before we replace things, we are just going round and doing the basics and the essentials, because we want to leave as much of the original material in place as we possibly can. We'll only replace the stone which is so badly decayed that you can't do anything with it.'

Dave Crouch climbs a rickety ladder up on to the roof of the church porch to help Andy Jacobs fit a solid square of honey- coloured stone into a hole above the window. The fit is millimetre perfect: 'It's good to think that we're working here today on this site and that, three hundred years ago, the old craftsmen were doing exactly the same thing in the same place with virtually the same tools as we're using today. All three of us are islanders and we set up our small business so that we could try and stay on the island and work as stonemasons. Our families go back for generations in this part of the world and, as long as there's stone masonry work to do here, we're very keen to be the ones who carry it out.' As he speaks, the new block of stone is mortared comfortably into place for another three hundred years.

Men have been producing glass for something like six thousand years and, at St Lawrence near Ventnor, members of the Harris family have been making their own colourful glassware since 1973. The equipment is modern but the skills and materials they use date back to thirteenth century Venice or third century Rome. Here they create local works of art, which are sold

Terry Heathcote

The view west from St Catherine's Point

Terry Heathcote

Dave Crouch (left) and Dave Hailstone (right), stonemasons

Terry Heathcote

Brook Chine, looking east to Freshwater

76

all over the world. The family glass-maker is Timothy Harris. He is a slight, dark-haired man with high cheekbones and spectacles, which are focused like laser beams on his work, which requires very high levels of concentration in the heat and the fire. His work produces dramatic mixes of hues – blues, greens, golds, reds, browns, silvers and yellows. There are wondrous seascapes and skyscapes with slashes of colour across dark backgrounds. Early in the process he sits on a stool, close to a raging furnace, rolling a red-hot football of glass on the end of a hollow, metal pole backwards and forwards across his asbestos-gloved hand. Slowly the early form of a vase begins to take shape: 'I went to college for a while. But I learnt most of my skills from being here since I was a boy. I began my early work when I was about seventeen – just assisting the glass-makers, cleaning irons, preparing work for the men, who were far more skilled and experienced than I was. From that basis I built my abilities up over the years – watching, absorbing what they did and learning more every day. That kind of teamwork and shared experience is important in this job because you need more than one person to make any single item.'

Timothy's tall, silent, crop-haired colleague coats the soft glass with what looks like blue paint powder and then, on top, with silver and gold leaf before plunging it back into the eye-searing heat of the furnace: 'A team of glass-makers can be anything from two to ten strong depending on the complexity of what they are making. Each of them has a different skill, so, within the group, everyone has his own, individual job.'

Hands twist and twist again rhythmically. Sweat pours down the men's faces but their eyes never waver. The pure silver melts itself into the molten glass, which is already tinged by the blue of the paint or dye. The vase-shaped bubble on the end of the iron rod is turned continually whether it is in or out of the heat: 'The ferocity of the furnace is something which you learn about very quickly. I've certainly burnt myself over the years and other glassmakers have too – not usually too badly. But you soon learn to respect the heat and the glass and to work with the material and not against it. It's obvious really. Anything that is glowing red or white in this place is generally pretty hot, so you learn to be careful with it and to treat it with caution. Having said that, it's vital that the glassmaker controls the glass and doesn't allow the glass to control him out of fear or anxiety.'

Next the vase-in-the-making has silver spines added to it as it is rolled backwards and forwards in a flat, barbecue pan. It addition there are what look like a scattering of green, white and black pebbles. They sink into the soft texture of the glass before it is poked back into the fire and the new ingredients are absorbed: 'All the glassmakers who work here live on the Isle of Wight, and most of them have come to us as boys from school or after graduating. Some have been here over twenty years, others just a few weeks and they are learning the trade from the bottom up. What you need is as wide a spread as you can find of experience, knowledge, learning and enthusiasm, which pleases our customers and which ensures a long-term continuity of excellence.'

A man, who looks like a boxer or a wrestler, blows down a lengthy tube into a bulging bubble of molten glass. The hope is that he will not blow too hard and explode the mass like a child's balloon. As the glass whirls and twirls a plume of purple fire from a flame-thrower explodes around it and follows it as it moves. Soon it begins to become recognisable as an exquisite and heavy, purple decorated jar: 'Glassmaking for me is not really a job. It's a passion. Glass has limitless possibilities and you never stop discovering new ones. That's why I find it so exciting.' In the window of the shop beside the workplace, scores of lovely pieces stand waiting for the customers to arrive, to admire and to buy.

Five generations of Sylvia Jones' family have farmed the fertile land just off the Military Road, Back of the Wight. Once they had a dairy herd, and Sylvia started milking by hand as a child. Today it is just arable and more famous as Dinosaur Farm, because in 1992, the island's largest one was found here! But, for Sylvia, it is her home – the only place on earth to be – with her chickens, her ducks, her sheep, her geese and her memories: 'I milked cows for sixty years, I did. And I did miles back home – we were brought up hard and rough in those days and no bad thing. And I used to say to Mum and Dad: 'Don't start milking too soon this afternoon. So they didn't begin till I got back home to do my bit of the milking and the cleaning up afterwards. I've always loved farm work. That's where my heart was all the time. I used to get up in the middle of the night if a cow was going to calve – never took any notice of what time it was. And I miss not having them today – though I have sheep and poultry and waterfowl to take their place. When we were buying cattle in those days, my Dad always used to tell me that, if ever I was going to buy a cow, I should always get it from along this southern coast of the Isle of Wight. They're bound to be strong along here because they have to withstand the weather – especially times like these.'

In every sense Syliva sums up the word, 'stalwart'. She wears an old, brown mac, hefty boots and a woolly, patterned hat. She has a ruddy, weather-beaten face and a quick and engaging smile. If there is such a thing as a Back of the Wight accent, she has it. She feeds corn to her ducks, geese and hens from a battered, metal bucket and talks to them the while. She stops by the stone barn where the remains of the dinosaur are housed. Her face is full of fun and her eyes of memories: 'I've had lots of strange and funny things happen to me in my time with animals on this farm. One day I went to fetch in the cows for milking, and one of them was by itself over the far side of the hill in a corner on her own. Now no farm animal is ever on its own unless there is something wrong with it. So I shouted over to her in my loudest voice: 'What the devil are you doing over there?' – and I got a noisy shout if I need it. So up popped a frightened head from the other side of the hedge and this man I'd never seen before said to me: "I'm only picking a few mushrooms." I never even knew he was there and he thought he was getting into trouble.' And her bright, merry, old face creases into the warmest of warm smiles.

Such a place is the southernmost sector of the Isle of Wight during a windswept January week towards the end of the twentieth century. Different months and different weathers would show it in other circumstances. But Dr G.C. Dunning in his history of Niton in 1951, compared the balmier spring and summer climate to the blasts of winter: 'St Catherine's Point has sterner moods when the wind howls round the old Oratory Tower up the hill, and the sea boils like the cauldrons of hell. Then this corner of the island speaks of its past, and the voice is eloquent of the history of England.' And W.H. Auden made something of the same point with his poem, 'On This Island':

> Look stranger on this island now
> The leaping light for your delight discovers
> Stand stable here
> And silent be
> That through the channels of the ear
> May wander like a river
> The swaying sound of the sea.

Harewood Forest

Harewood Forest, old enough to be recorded in Domesday Book of 1086, lies a couple of miles to the east of Andover, in northern Hampshire. The upper waters of the great River Test – one of the country's finest trout streams – mark its eastern boundary, and bourns and tributaries that run into and feed the river surround the woodland. Kings and queens used to hunt here, and the place is steeped in ancient history and an association with such distant names as Edgar, Ethelred, Edward, Ethelwold, Ethelwolf, Aelfrith and Elfrida. Murder and intrigue, mistresses and betrayal, violence and deception are part and parcel of the forest's folklore. In fact it is not at all unlike the behaviour of the powers that be at the end of the twentieth century. But, history aside, this is above all fine country for farmers, for walkers, for fishermen and for those who want to get away from it all or would like to enjoy lovely churches and secluded villages with welcoming pubs. Even in the bleak days of a cold, February week there is plenty to admire among the forest trees and tracks and on the still, green meadows of the Test valley. And, with winter holding its icy grip and blizzards blocking the narrow lanes, for a little while yet there is the possibility of solitude and peace – undisturbed by the madding crowd of fair-weather visitors.

Harewood Forest sheltered an ammunition dump during the Second World War. Nowadays, thank heavens, it has returned to its peaceful origins and woodsmen Ricky Bolam from Wherwell and his partner, Ray Edmunds, work among the trees as such men have for centuries gone. Ricky has been toiling in the woods since he was fifteen years old and in Harewood Forest for twenty-five years. There is more than enough for the two men to do on their six hundred acres of woodland – even on the bleakest February day: 'I've worked in the woods all of my working life with the exception of two years' national service. That's getting on for forty-five years now. And my father was a forester before me in the North of England, so I suppose you could say that it's in the blood. This type of wood is particularly good to work in. It's ancient woodland – mainly oak. It's not a forest that's been grown in rows and rows of trees. It's natural woodland that is meant to be natural. It's not a place you want to mess about with too much. We thin it. We take small circles of trees out from time to time to encourage butterflies and things like that. We keep it tidy and we harvest timber and firewood.'

There is a bonfire blazing in a clearing as the two men clear trees and branches, fallen and broken by the winter gales. A powdering of snow covers the rides and the clearings. Beneath his hard hat, Ricky has a strong and serious face but with smile creases round his eyes, which don't tell lies. In his voice there is an attractive mixture of Hampshire and his father's North Country. While the men work, a slim fallow deer crosses a snowy forest track and pauses, one forefoot lifted, gazing at them fearlessly: 'We like to see the deer and the other animals that live here – foxes, badgers, all kinds of birds. We encourage those. And the forest and the wildlife jog along happily together so long as we can protect the young trees from squirrels and, of course, from the deer as well.'

Ricky is energetically sawing up a fallen silver birch, his chainsaw revving and barking and shattering the peace of the forest. His hands are well gloved against the biting cold: 'In the winter, of course, a lot of firewood goes out for sale from here. To supply it we try to stick to blown-down trees if we can or to birches, of which we have an abundance. So, hopefully, between them we can leave the good stands of oaks alone and concentrate on getting the poor stuff out.'

The two woodsmen move on to a giant sawbench and circular saw with dinosaur-sized teeth beside piles of logs and heavy timber in the middle of a wintery ride: 'When we're

The River Test near Wherwell

80

cutting with the circular saw – planks, fence posts or railings – the way you do it varies, because you get some wood that is very tight-grained, which means that you have to work extra hard to get through it.' The tractor-driven blade strains and slows as it bites into the hard wood: 'That's why we use the wedges to open up the cut as the blade goes through. Push or hammer them in and it opens it up a bit and makes life easier for the saw. I get a heck of a lot of satisfaction from what I'm doing. I enjoy my work. I believe that most people that tried it would too. All right, you've got to get your hands dirty. You've got to work hard. But it's such a release after what other people go through – commuting, riding the motorways, office work. Town life, I just don't think I could put up with it. No, I don't think I could live in a city or work there.'

At lunchtime Ricky heads back through the forest down towards the Test to make sure that his pride and joy, two of his unusual mottled-grey horses, are coping all right with the frozen land and the snowy conditions and to take them a bit of grub: 'I was brought up as a child with horses. Then I never saw another one from the age of fifteen. Well, much later on, my daughter wanted to ride, so she went off to a riding school. Next, of course, my children all got the bug and they wanted to have their own horses. And it has escalated from there. Now we've got four. It makes me a very poor man, but also a very happy one. I love 'em.' And he stands and watches with pleasure as the big beasts munch their hay on the snow-covered grass. Below, the great river moves slowly southwards – the sounds of its pouring waters clear to hear and its banks rich with the movement of birds and wildlife.

Sheep have grazed the clearings of Harewood Forest back into the mists of time. Today, it is all on a larger scale and John Read, whose ewes will soon be lambing, looks after his flock beside the Test and just below the woods at Wherwell. Their location demands a daily two-way journey across a ford in the river with food, hay, dogs and equipment. To add to the problems there is a blizzard blowing snow parallel to the ground, and three-foot snowdrifts. It is a magnificent winter scene. Overhead, flocks of swans are gliding and honking as they sweep in to land on the water with elegant grace: 'The snow gives no difficulties to the sheep at all. As long as you keep them well and regularly fed, they'll normally go and find shelter from the weather. So it doesn't cause them any great discomfort. The rain is a lot worse. That takes more energy out of them. They start lambing in about five weeks and I've just begun feeding them concentrates. In addition, they get as much hay as they want. And, during the next week or two, I'll start building up the concentrates, so that they'll have good, strong lambs and plenty of milk for them.'

While his two sheepdogs look on from the back of the trailer, John trudges through the snow turning over the metal feed troughs, which are frozen upside down to the ground. The sheep mill around as they wait impatiently: 'I don't think sheep are stupid at all. They've got strong instincts, which they've built up over hundreds of years. Those instincts have kept them going for a million years, perhaps, and they still keep them alive today. Sheep are sensible enough to follow one another in lines up on the hills or down here in the valley. The ones that didn't follow probably fell into the bogs and drowned. So there are good, historical reasons why they've got these instincts. The main thing about farming sheep is to use their intuitions to make life as easy as possible for me and for the sheep themselves.'

At long last John returns to the trailer and takes down paper sacks of sheep nuts and barley to pour into the waiting feeders. The sound of the food hitting the metal as the wind howls is like a children's orchestra. The dogs, by the magic that they possess, hold back the ravenous flock until John has finished: 'The collies are an important part of the operation. They give me independence. With their help, there's nothing I can't do with a flock of sheep. If I've got to move them I can do that. If I need to catch individuals because they are lame I can get the dogs to hold the flock back and get hold of them safely. When I put out the feed, particularly in these conditions when the sheep are so hungry from the cold, if the dogs didn't hold them the sheep would mob me and chances are I would be tripped up and knocked over. A big bunch of animals

An evocative road through Harewood Forest

82

like that, tons of weight between them and pressing so hard for their grub, makes a frightening force and weight. And, when you are down, there's nothing much you can do about it with the whole mass of sheep about you. So, without the dogs, this part of the job would be impossible. In fact, without them, I'd probably work in an office.' He doesn't mean it, of course, and he smiles as he watches his hungry horde at their meal. Now and again their eyes look up to him briefly as if in appreciation. With the dogs it is more like adoration. And John moves on and loads bales of sweet-smelling summer hay into metal lockers from which the sheep, which have had their fill of concentrates, can now help themselves to a second course: 'In fact, there's no way I'd work in the town now, although I was brought up there. I've become a country boy and that's what I'm going to stay.' The wind blows the reeds flat against the water. A moorhen scuttles through the sedge. More snow is on the way. The banks of the Test are pure white against the black of the rippled water.

In distant days it is certain that Harewood Forest stretched well beyond its present boundaries. It is unlikely that it reached quite as far away as Stoke – four miles to the north – and absolutely certain that it did not shelter Kune Kune pigs, though it would have been home to plenty of wild boar. Angela Blake, who comes originally from Hamburg, in Germany, and who wanted, as a child, to be an elephant keeper at the famous zoo there, keeps geese, Maori Kune Kune pigs from New Zealand, and plenty of other animals too on her smallholding at Stoke. She has, for the time being, had to forgo the challenge of elephants: 'The geese were among the first arrivals here. We got them soon after we arrived. We had a spate of burglaries in the village and we decided that we were not going to be one of the victims. So we bought the geese and they seem to have done the job. They've actually seen off some strangers who were prowling about.' The geese are as white as the snow which surrounds them, as they squabble over a tub of water big enough to contain just one of their number. Nearby, some slim, pitch-black sheep, the rams with curly horned heads, make sharp silhou-ettes against the white background: 'The Hebridean sheep came to us last April when a friend of ours, who owned them, moved house and didn't know what to do with them. They knew we had some grass and asked us if we could look after them for a while. We agreed and they seem to have stayed and multiplied since then. But they are no trouble at all to look after really.'

In addition to the geese and the sheep, there is a collection of various hens, ducks and bantams. They include some distinguished-looking cocks and hens with white badges, like ear muffs, on either side of their heads: 'These are Old English pheasant fowl. I got them at the same time as I started with the Kune Kune pigs. They are strong characters. They absolutely refuse to use the hutch which we made for them. As soon as we shut them up in it overnight and then let them out in the morning, they decided that the tree was a much better option for them and they've been living up in its branches ever since.'

Angela carries a bale of straw to one of the arcs in her snow-clad, frozen and muddy paddock. The startled and smiling face of a chubby black-and-white hairy pig emerges and greets her like the good friend that she is. Angela continues with her perfect English, which is attached to a charming German accent: 'Kune Kune pigs were the Maori village pigs. They were principally kept for meat. In 1972 they were "discovered" by the agriculture ministry in New Zealand and it was found that only a few were left. One of the officials managed to persuade eighteen of the Maoris to sell him their pigs, though they were reluctant to part with them, which I can quite understand. And he started a breeding herd. Today there are over a thousand Kune Kunes over there, so he has done a good job.' As she speaks, two more stout, black-and-white speckled pigs come out of the sty, blinking painfully in the bright sunlight reflecting off the snow. They look like porcine versions of Friesian or Holstein cattle, though much hairier: 'They are great fun to be with. They just adore people. They seem to want to be around humans all the time. In fact they get upset if you don't go and see them and stroke them, scratch their backs and give them a treat when you are walking past.'

Angela's nine-year-old son Sebastian appears from a smaller arc in the next-door paddock, where he is spending time with his friend and pet pig, which he grooms and lies in the straw with as one would with the best of one's chums: 'He loves the pigs. Spotty is his favourite and he spends hours with him. If I don't know where Sebastian is, I just have to go down to the meadow and look in the sties and, nine times out of ten, he's there covered in straw and, often as not, asleep beside his pig.' Spotty is a small, even hairier version of his parents and is busy nuzzling his pal's face and taking half a carrot from his mouth. The boar and the sow look on enviously from next door, their jaws chomping on the new straw: 'One of the interesting things about Kune Kunes is that they are grass-eaters, and they thrive on grass. So, if you have a quarter of an acre of meadow, you have everything you need for a Kune Kune pig. Add to that, if you can, an apple orchard and they will be one hundred per cent happy with the windfalls added to the grass. So they are cheap to keep. And this weather is no problem for them either. In fact all our animals seem to like the snow and the pigs in particular. When it first started snowing we let them out and they jumped up and down and played with it, and

Angela Blake and her Maori Kune Kune pigs

were trying to catch the falling flakes. They didn't quite know what to make of it, but it gave them great amusement.'

At the end of February, the trout-fishing season is not many weeks away, so this is an important time of the year for Head River Keeper Bill Hawkins from Wherwell and his friend and colleague, John Colley. The Test is host each year to some of the most demanding fishermen in the world, and now is the time to cut weeds, clear banks, mend bridges and tidy beats in good time for their arrival. Wild brown trout fishing, with all its skills and subtleties, is the name of the game: 'The job as underkeeper – trout and salmon – was advertised in a magazine. I applied and I got it and I've been here over twenty-five years now. I think it's a wonderful job – a beautiful way of life.'

Bill has a narrow, thoughtful face with prominent cheek-bones. There is no spare flesh on him. He has not yet lost his Yorkshire accent and he works with a venerable metal-stemmed pipe clenched between his teeth. Both men are in waders and up to their knees in the tumbling river water. They wield old-fashioned scythes and move rhythmically in line abreast downstream cutting away the green undergrowth on the river bed. It grows thickly, over-fertilised as it is by the nitrogen leaching off the cereal fields upstream, getting into the water, encouraging the weeds and doing God knows what to fish and to human beings: 'We cut the weeds this time of the year so that the winter water washes the bed of the river and then the weed that comes on in the spring is clean and fresh for the fish and what they feed on. If you're in the stream working, even in this sort of icy weather, your feet are still warmer than your hands. You see, the water temperature will always be warmer than the air temperature.' The severed weeds drift away downstream on the current. A heron, spooked by the unusual bundles heading its way, scuttles off into the late afternoon sky. Swans soar and whistle overhead with their heavy, drum-beat wings: 'In February, we're also tidying up the banks and cutting the limbs off trees, which get in the way of the fishermen on the footpath or overhang the river too much. This is the time of year for odd jobs and tidy-

Bill Hawkins, river keeper, selecting fishing flies

growth on the trees along the bank. Snow tumbles down on their heads from the branches as they fall. There is a bonfire nearby, which the men are tempted to linger over as they drag the wood to it and throw it on top: 'I suppose I was nine or ten years old when I first started fishing. My brother was a keen fisherman and I used to go with him. He bought me a little fishing-rod as a present and I used to catch small gudgeon and roach with it. And I've still got that rod. Well, I expect that I've progressed a bit since then and I hope I can be considered a fair fisherman now. And that, of course, is important for this job. From 1 May, when we put the new trout in the Test, up until July, the fishing is not too difficult in this river. But from then onwards the fish become what we call 'educated' and they are very hard to catch. And that's when the men get sorted out from the boys.' The smoke from the fire drifts away swiftly in the brisk wind from the north-east. It travels parallel to the snow and soon seems to become part of it as it sinks down towards it – white on white.

At Mayfield Farm, the fat white ducks seem to be enjoying everything that the February weather can throw at them as they prattle and paddle in the puddles and on the grass. The resident boxers prefer the warmth of their house at Binley as they peer suspiciously from the farmhouse windows. But they seem contented as well. It is not so good for the horses, though, in the mud and cold of their winter meadows. But spring is not far away and it is time for Cynthia Sheerman to get her horses' training under way, ready for the kinder weather ahead and the shows that go with it. Cynthia rode her first point-to-point in 1947 without even walking the course and, today, stalwart that she is, she has taught herself random driving – that is, three horses in a line. This is a major hand- and finger-wrenching challenge. But, with that amount of horsepower, she could be in Harewood Forest, a few miles to the south, in no time: 'During the war I was in the Land Army, milking cows mainly and delivering milk in a float with a cob. Well, the cob was new and so was I. So we always got lost and as a result I was late for the afternoon milking

ing up in general, weather always permitting. But I suppose if it permits today with all this snow on the ground and ice on the water, it will permit most things most days.'

A chainsaw crackles into life as Bill and John tackle the

Cynthia Sheerman

*Cynthia Sheerman, horsewoman, random driving
(three horses in a line)*

and missed it.'

Cynthia cautiously navigates the narrow, icy lanes. It is a question whether or not she should take to the tarmac in such conditions. When the first horse comes to a junction it is impossible for Cynthia, on the driver's pillion, to see whether there is anything coming along the main road. She drives the three bay horses with care and consideration, a cheeky cap perched on her head, not a tremor in her voice but great concentration on her experienced face: 'This rig has the same amount of reins as a six-in-hand – and that's a lot of leather to hold on to. But it's harder because, driving three pairs at once, the leaders keep one another straight, whereas, when you have them in one, long, thin line they can whip round on you. The lead horse is twenty-five and he was bred by Lady Coleman, who put him in a sale as a foal, and he made sixty-five guineas to the gypsies. They broke him in and he was sold at Wickham gypsy fair. I stood by and saw him that day and said, 'One day I'll own you'. Ginger is the middle horse.

He was on his way to Southampton market to go on the horse-meat lorry. The truck transporting him broke down and the chap went for help at a dealer's yard. He was asked there whether he'd got any driving horses on board and he said, 'Yes, this one'. So Ginger ended up at the yard and, from then on, he was sold many, many times. So when I bought him I called him Ginger because he had had a rough time like Black Beauty's Ginger. And the third one is my new baby. He is seven. I've had him a couple of seasons for showing, but I'm more frightened of driving him singly than I am of driving all three of them together. I'd never sell any of them because of what might happen to them with a new owner. No horse will ever go out alive from here. They are all provided for if I go first. I love them and the reason I put them and myself through the complications of this three-in-a-line driving is for the excitement – the adrenaline kick. I'm always frightened up here, but I wouldn't do it if I wasn't scared. That's invigorating you see. I mean, what else can an old lady do for thrills?' The three matching horses with their handsome carriage and gallant driver disappear down the snow-bound track, their hoof-beats echoing on and endlessly on into the distance. Overhead, the February sky is grey verging on black.

There is no missing the large, metal sign of a perky blacksmith with hammer raised ready for action outside the two-hundred-year-old forge at St Mary Bourne, and customers come from all over the area round Harewood Forest to benefit from the skills of Len Mew and his brother, the village blacksmiths. They took the job on from their father, keep a few sheep behind the workshops and specialise in wrought-iron work, welding, mending and making farm machinery and any other tricky jobs that come their way. Len has been here for forty years now: 'I started in 1959 and we did shoe some horses then. But they dwindled off over the next twenty years or so and now we don't do any at all. With this job you have to keep a constant eye on the heat of the fire because, with the mild steel they send you nowadays, you can soon burn and

Len Mew, blacksmith

works, he still thinks of and remembers the good old times: 'I can recall the smell of the hot metal burning into the horses' hooves – a lovely smell. Once you've smelt it, you never forget it and it brings back such good memories of those quieter times. Nothing quite like that today. I'm building a fireplace – and that's good work, but not so romantic perhaps. But there is still a pleasure in keeping the workshop going because the old skills are gradually disappearing now and there's not many that's going to take on this kind of job. I wouldn't ever want to move away from here – my home and my work. Not even if I got the six numbers on the lottery I wouldn't. Nothing would drag me from this valley. It's just the right place to be.'

In 1822 William Cobbett rode through Harewood Forest on his sturdy and patient horse and wrote:

spoil the metal. With the old iron, in the days when I began to work, you could get that to a white heat and still use it effectively. But with today's soft steel the end will drop off if you get it too hot.'

Len is hard at work on some intricate, curled decorations for a cast-iron fireplace for a local farmhouse. He has a serious face, strong arms, iron grey hair and a warm, Hampshire accent. His frame has been toughened by decades of hard, physical work. Sweat mottles his forehead as he pokes into the coals and then carries the searing metal to the anvil. As he

The country, though so open, has its beauties. The homesteads in the sheltered bottoms with fine, lofty trees about the houses and yards, form a beautiful contrast with the large, open fields. The little villages running straggling along the dells – always with tall trees and rookeries – are very interesting objects, even in the winter. You feel a sort of satisfaction, when you are out upon the bleak hills yourself, at the thought of the shelter which is experienced in the dwellings below you in the valleys.

Cottages in Wherwell village

88

End Piece

Home for me is in Hampshire's New Forest. Perched on top of a low hill in a plain old cottage and surrounded by my few acres and a wood, I have found my small piece of paradise in a wicked world. It is worth more to me than a lottery win, any title that the Queen can offer or even the gift of immortality. And so it is, I believe, for many who have the good fortune to live in these privileged southern counties. The rich and the famous may do as they please. The power-hungry, who run our nations and our town halls, can cause what chaos they wish. And the academics and intellectuals who feel so superior to the rest of the human race can continue to look down their noses at me and mine. I shall go on living my quiet and contented life surrounded by what is, to me, the finest scenery and the best environment anywhere in the world. In 1858, Thomas Hughes, the author of *Tom Brown's School Days*, wrote about his special part of the South Country – The Vale of the White Horse in Royal Berkshire: 'Most of you have probably travelled down the Great Western Railway as far as Swindon. Those of you who did so with their eyes open have been aware, soon after leaving Didcot station, of a fine range of chalk hills running parallel with the railway on the left-hand side as you go down, and distant some two or three miles, more or less, from the line. The highest point in the range is the White Horse Hill, which you come in front of just before you stop at the Shrivenham station. If you love English scenery and have a few hours to spare, you can't do better, the next time you pass, than to stop at the Farringdon Road or Shrivenham station, and make your way to that highest point. And those who care for the vague old stories that haunt countrysides all about England will not, if they are wise, be content with only a few hours' stay: for, glorious as the view is, the neighbourhood is yet more interesting for its relics of bygone times. I only know two English neighbourhoods thoroughly and in each, within a circle of five miles, there is enough of interest and beauty to last any reasonable man his life.'

What a lesson for our footloose, impatient and dissatisfied age, with so many of us rushing around, traversing the globe and demanding more and richer experiences in ever shorter time-spans. The Holy Grail we are seeking may be closer at hand than we ever dreamt – and nowhere near Heathrow Airport, the European Union headquarters in Brussels or on the slopes of Machu Picchu. It might just be here in dear old, overlooked southern England.

About the Author

Farmer's son, Anthony Howard, has lived on a smallholding in the north of Hampshire's New Forest with his wife, Elisabeth, and a few sheep and chickens since 1965. His three children, Katie, Tom and Emma grew up here and now all work in London in broadcasting and journalism. When he can tear himself away from his home, he writes, produces and directs films and other programmes for British television. Over the years he has worked on some 3000 hours of drama, light entertainment, musicals, talks, documentaries and factual programmes. He also writes books about the English countryside and a column for a magazine. The *Country Ways* series was a project which he was originally saving up for his retirement – if he could find a broadcaster kind enough to commission it. Events intervened and it first went into production in 1983. Now, sixteen years on and two hundred films later, it is probably the longest-running regional documentary series in the country.